DanishModern

Danish Modern

ANDREW HOLLINGSWORTH

GIBBS SMITH
TO ENRICH AND INSPIRE HUMANKIND

Salt Lake City │ Charleston │ Santa Fe │ Santa Barbara

To my mother, who inspired my love for design and antiques; Linda and Gail,
who gave me the courage to pursue my passion professionally; all of my wonderful
clients, whose shared passion and support give each day meaning; and finally,
my life partner, Gilles, who suffers through the never-ending home redecorating
necessary to accommodate my latest finds.

First Edition
12 11 10 09 08   5 4 3 2 1

Text © 2008 Andrew Hollingsworth
Photographs © 2008 Scott Thompson, except as noted below
Photographs © 2008 Egon Douglas on pages 14, 21, 22, 40, 44 (bottom), 45, 49 (bottom),
59, 64, 71, 73, 77, 82, 90, 91, 92, 101, 102, 104, 111, 115, 124, 125, 126, 136, 137,
158, 159, 160, 161, 201, 204, 206, 208, 209, 227. Photographs © 2008 David Rosenthall
on pages 27, 32 (top), 35 (top), 51, 53, 76, 128, 129, 131, 207, 210, 211 (top), 212.
Photographs © 2008 Matthew Millman on pages 106, 133, 184, 185. Photographs © 2008
Andrew Hollingsworth on pages 15, 32 (bottom), 44 (top), 95, 211 (middle).

Published by
Gibbs Smith, Publisher
P.O. Box 667
Layton, Utah 84041

1.800.835.4993 orders
www.gibbs-smith.com

Designed and produced by Adrienne Pollard
Printed and bound in China
Gibbs Smith books are printed on either recycled,
100% post consumer waste, or FSC certified papers.

Library of Congress Cataloging-in-Publication Data

Hollingsworth, Andrew.
  Danish modern / Andrew Hollingsworth. — 1st ed.
    p. cm.
  ISBN-13: 978-1-58685-811-7
  ISBN-10: 1-58685-811-4
  1. Furniture—Denmark—History—20th century. 2. Modernism (Aesthetics)—Denmark.
I. Title.
  NK2585.H65 2008
  749.09489'0904—dc22
                        2008018002

Acknowledgments

No book of this nature can be written without great indebtedness to the many people who assisted me. My greatest thanks go to my assistant, Alexis Kowalsky, without whose help I might never have made it to the finish line. And then to my publicist, Susan Bishopric, whose work led to a seemingly random visit from Gibbs Smith, my publisher, who saw the local write-up of my exhibition on Borge Mogensen. And many, many thanks to the following: my editor, Lisa Anderson, whose patience was tested more times than I care to admit; my publisher for having confidence in a small, unknown shop owner; my photographers who brought the book to life, but especially Scott Thompson, who went the extra mile; the very supportive library staff at the Danish Museum of Decorative Arts in Copenhagen; Svenskform; Trapholt Museum; Fredericia Furniture; Fritz Hansen Furniture; Rudolf Rasmussen Cabinetmakers; Finn Rasmussen; and all of the clients, decorators, and others who supported the effort.

Contents

One of the most iconic chairs of the twentieth century, designed for the Royal SAS Hotel, Copenhagen.
Arne Jacobsen Egg Chair and Ottoman of fabric and cast aluminum, 1958. Manufactured by Fritz Hansen.

Introduction:
The Appeal *of* Danish Modern

Despite its name, Danish Modern in many ways transcends the word *modern*—it is a style that can be incorporated successfully into contemporary and traditional interiors, urban and country alike, lending itself to a timeless and universal appeal. Its forms range from those inspired by the great traditions of furniture making in the ancient world to free flowing organic shapes that seem to define the twentieth century. Its materials range from lighter, more casual woods like European oak to rich, deep woods like Brazilian rosewood. It is a style that yields both production pieces and those made individually by some of the greatest cabinet-makers of all time. Considering these characteristics, the beauty and broad appeal of Danish Modern cannot be overstated.

A Danish Modern chair with Chinese influence. Ole Wanscher ladder-back chair of Brazilian rosewood and leather, circa 1942. Manufactured by A. J. Iversen.

Facing: The craft of Modernism: natural simplicity. Danish Modern lounge chair with collection of Danish ceramics in the foreground.

Indeed, Danish Modern has undergone a global resurgence of interest in the last decade or so as Modernism itself has been rediscovered and the accomplishments in design and furniture making of Denmark and other Scandinavian countries have been recognized. In the United States, demand was initially driven by discovery of those iconic modern pieces that were mass imported or manufactured in the States by great architects/designers like Hans Wegner, Finn Juhl, and Arne Jacobsen. As the style's appeal has expanded and evolved, discriminating collectors are increasingly seeking out prototypes, unique and limited production pieces made by the collaboration of top designers and cabinetmakers/manufacturers of the period such as Kaare Klint and Rudolf Rasmussen, Ole Wanscher and A. J. Iversen, Borge Mogensen and Fredericia, and Poul Kjaerholm and E. Kold Christensen. As can be expected, values have risen over the last several years, but, with the exception of Poul Kjaerholm, Danish Modern remains highly affordable compared to other modern and historical design styles. Indeed, many limited production pieces of incredible quality can be found for prices similar to that of new furniture purchased in "to the trade" or designer showrooms across the U.S. In a nod to the timelessness of these pieces, licensed manufacturers have begun reissuing the most iconic pieces, while others have begun copying or using the designs as inspiration.

What has fueled this interest and why is Danish Modern still relevant? Fashion, to be sure, plays a part, but the roots go even deeper. Much of what was produced in Denmark in the mid-twentieth century grew out of centuries-old traditions of cabinetmaking in that country. While the Danes employed modern methods of production, they did so on a limited scale appropriate for a small country perched on the northern edge of Europe. Much of the country's furniture, while modern in line and scale, is rooted in the historical development of form and is thus able to transcend time, incorporating seamlessly into today's interiors. From 1930 through 1970, the Danes infused the best of European historical design, along with ancient Greek, Egyptian, and Asian forms, in an understated, matter-of-fact way reflective of their cultural identity and craftsman traditions. The result was a prolific renaissance of style, quality, and sophistication that is still only beginning to be appreciated in the homes of twenty-first-century America.

What Is Modern(ism)?

Most stories of the development of twentieth-century design focus on the advent of technology and industrialization in bringing "good" design to the public at affordable prices. The elimination of ornament, the advent of the designer, and the obsolescence of traditional craftsmanship coincided, as the expanding middle classes required more and more goods of industrialized quality. Simply put, the stories tell how Modernism, a movement loosely defined as breaking with classic or traditional forms, grew out of the ashes of nineteenth-century Victorian excesses of style and flourished through the post–World War II boom period. Globally, this period covers a wide range of national/regional movements responding to local markets (see facing page).

While mostly national in genesis and interpretation, the ideas and concepts of these movements spread throughout Europe and North America. Despite the pretenses, some embraced the democratic ideals of design for the masses more than others whose concepts and applications were more elitist than populist.

In colloquial terms, the words "modern," "contemporary," and "modernism" seem to be used interchangeably and basically mean clean lines and unadulterated, simple forms when they refer to the decorative arts. A dictionary may define "modern" as meaning something like "relating to the present or recent times as opposed to the remote past." Perhaps because many of us have lived during the modern age itself, we are only beginning to be far enough away technologically from it to make sense of the period.

Danish Modern
(1930–1970) overlaps
many of the other
movements of the
twentieth century.

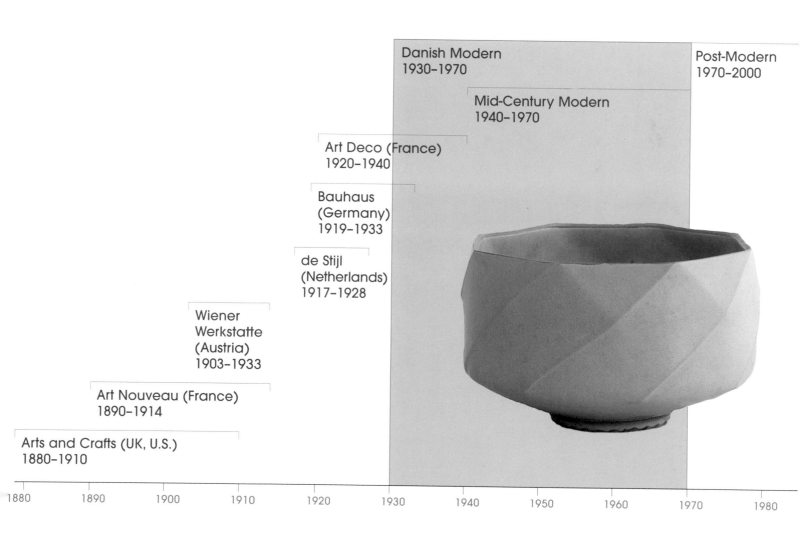

Danish Modern
1930–1970

Post-Modern
1970–2000

Mid-Century Modern
1940–1970

Art Deco (France)
1920–1940

Bauhaus
(Germany)
1919–1933

de Stijl
(Netherlands)
1917–1928

Wiener
Werkstatte
(Austria)
1903–1933

Art Nouveau (France)
1890–1914

Arts and Crafts (UK, U.S.)
1880–1910

1880   1890   1900   1910   1920   1930   1940   1950   1960   1970   1980

What Is Danish Modern?

When people refer to Scandinavian design, what they are usually referring to is a look represented by a set of aesthetic and functional design values associated with the products of five countries—Denmark, Sweden, Norway, Finland, and Iceland—in the twentieth century. Each country has its own history and evolution of design, with distinct preferences and intraregional rivalries. Up until the twentieth century, all mostly imported and copied the best of European and Asian design, although they took their cues from different places at different times and applied their own unique senses of style. The Swedes, for example, took inspira-

An early Danish Modern example of a classic, elegant form reduced to its simplest extreme. Birch and silk armchair with double-caned back, 1928. Manufactured by cabinetmaker Jorgen Christensen.

tion from the French in the development of their eighteenth-century Gustavian style of painted furniture and lighter woods, while the Danes were drawn to the classicism of English furniture and the deep, richer look of mahogany. The Modernist approach in these countries grew out of those traditions. Rather than rejecting the history of design, like their European counterparts, the first wave of modernist designers and cabinetmakers in Scandinavia embraced its historical framework, prototypes, and traditions of joinery while applying modern lines and tools. As the movement progressed, others took from those historical traditions the concepts of quality and craftsmanship in a more industrialized fashion while dismissing the more obvious historical prototyping for freer, more organic forms. The combination of both of these streams of design consciousness ultimately secured the universal appeal of Scandinavian design and its place in history. With rare exception, it was a style that was never too far out or inaccessible for most to appreciate; indeed, its reemergence in recent years confirms a timelessness that we associate with classics.

Aino Aalto leather wing-back chair with birch legs, Finland, 1940s.

All of the Scandinavian countries made contributions to the mid-century movement we call Scandinavian Modern, but Denmark has a special place as a center of intense and prolific design. This book addresses the birth and growth of Danish Modern within the context of Scandinavian Modern and the global Modernism movement as a whole. It is not meant as an academic treatise but rather an introductory text to a specific area of Nordic design: Danish Modern furniture as the outgrowth of movements originating in Europe in the early twentieth century. Discussion of Swedish design is briefly entertained for the sake of comparison purposes and because the two countries, while having their own design histories, have became so intertwined, and sometimes outright confused, in our American understanding of the subject. While Finnish furniture design is not addressed, its contribution to twentieth-century design is unquestioned. Three notable examples from the period are Eero Saarinen, the Finnish architect who immigrated to the United States (he designed the Tulip table and chairs among other things); Alvar Aalto, who founded the company Artek and whose molded wood chairs are similarly iconic; and Tapio Wirkkala, who produced works of great beauty inspired by nature. Norway and Iceland were much smaller players in the development of Modern furniture. The influence of Norway on modern furniture design was relatively small, although designers such as Alfred Sture produced some interesting work during this period.

In its 1982 survey exhibition and catalogue, the Cooper-Hewitt Museum defined Scandinavian Modern as the period 1880–1980, or shortly before the end of the Victorian period through the time of the exhibit. More recently, the Victoria and Albert Museum (the V&A) Modernism exhibition in 2006 dated the global Modernism movement from 1914–1939 with 1930 being the starting point in Scandinavia. That was the year of the great Stockholm Exhibition, and it is certainly a critical juncture for what would evolve into what we now know as Scandinavian Modern, a period when the Scandinavians captured the world's attention with their innovative designs of uncompromising quality. This definition is appropriate and reflective of the current meaning of the word *Modernism* (linked to the de Stijl/Bauhaus period). For the purposes of this book, I will use 1930 as the starting point and extend the Scandinavian or Danish term through Mid-Century Modern and the Pop Period to around 1970.

This book will take you on a journey that you may not have traveled, as the path we take discusses not the mass-market design we came to singularly associate with Danish Modern furniture in the U.S., but the work of designers and cabinetmakers whose unapologetic attention to craftsmanship and quality played an integral part in the development of the overall movement. It will also illustrate through photography the reemergence of the Nordic aesthetic into contemporary American homes and provide reference tools for understanding the current market, caring for the furniture, and learning more about the period.

Let the story begin.

Facing: Frits Henningsen easy chair of leather and mahogany, circa 1930s.

Danish Modern Furniture:
Roots *and* Development

Developments leading to what we now know and refer to as the Danish Modern style can be divided as follows: 1770–1916, when the general traditions of Danish cabinetmaking, style, and taste were established; 1917–1945, when those traditions began to be modernized by a very charismatic and influential chairman of the Royal Danish Academy of Arts' new furniture department; and, finally, 1946–1967, when the idealism of the post–World War II boom aligned with these developments to create a new global sensation in style.

Throughout these periods, but particularly in the twentieth century, there was an interesting interplay of government, industry, and museums in the promotion and encouragement of design. The level of cooperation among these institutions evolved in a synergistic way to encourage and reinforce an appreciation for the importance of design in society and human development. If today's technological advancements are largely defined and communicated through high technology and the Internet, those of the twentieth century were defined by new industrial, political, and social possibilities manifested through newfangled designs for the growing middle classes. The new products generated during the period were communicated to the public at large-scale exhibitions and fairs. The profusion and magnitude of these exhibits, the level of interest and attendance at them, and their importance in promoting industry were instrumental in conveying progress and promoting the material benefits of modernism at a time when the ubiquitous televisions and computers of today's age did not exist. We will take a look at a number of the key exhibits in Europe and the U.S. as they fed off of each other in many ways.

1770–1916:
Establishing a Tradition

The Danish tradition of quality craftsmanship was encouraged through the establishment of the Cabinetmakers' Guild in the sixteenth century and the Royal Danish Academy of Arts in the eighteenth century. In the nineteenth century, as industrialization took root, cooperative societies were formed and ideas of modern social democratization and design surfaced. These developments would provide the traditions and formative concepts that would prove critical in the twentieth century.

Danish Cabinetmakers' Guild

The Danish Cabinetmakers' Guild was established in 1554 as a trade association to protect and promote the Danish cabinetmaking industry. Just over two hundred years later, in 1770, a regulation was enacted to establish the Royal Danish Academy of Arts to train apprentice craftsmen in drawing and to inspect and approve masterpieces. Up until the eighteenth century, Denmark had relied upon imports and copies of French design. The guild proposed the establishment of

Danish Modern easy
chair with classic English
influence. Frits Henningsen
wingback easy chair of
leather and mahogany,
circa 1930s.

tariffs so the cabinetmakers might compete more favorably with the French, but
the government, in its wisdom, chose instead to stimulate demand for English
styles. That understated English style, employing beautifully carved if simple
forms, thereafter became the model for the Danish cabinetmaking industry.

In 1777, the Danish Furniture Stores were founded by the state to advise,
support, and educate furniture craftsmen. In addition to selling the cabinetmaker's

Early Danish Modern easy chair with an air of the Arts and Crafts movement. Mogens Voltelen's Copenhagen Chair of mahogany and leather, 1936. Manufactured by Niels Vodder.

goods, the stores provided an educational source as well as operational funding and support and served as a means through which to supply craftsmen with designers. Trained in England, these designers were instrumental in promulgating the new English aesthetic. Some of the masters of this period are considered to be Bindesboll, Abildgaard, Brotterup, and Hansen, and their works are still highly regarded and sought after in Denmark today. The guild stores operated successfully up until the early nineteenth century.

Danish Cooperative Society and
Late Nineteenth-Century Idealism

In response to the demand for furniture for the expanding middle class, the Association of Danish Cooperative Societies, or Farmers Co-op, was founded in 1880 to distribute and sell furniture and other household goods. During this period, theorists in Scandinavian countries were beginning to reevaluate issues of national identity as well as to recognize the need for social equality. There was a growing movement to encourage designers and artists to embrace national traditions in recognition of the idea that "to be significant, design must be an outgrowth of the fundamental values of a society, and that the role of the artist/craftsman is to manifest such values through the creative process."[1]

Contemporary philosophers and art historians saw the fine and decorative arts as a necessary part of the education of the public for the betterment of society. A major proponent of the burgeoning Arts and Crafts movement in Scandinavia was Lorentz Dietrichsen, who implored, "It is very important for a people's national consciousness that art and 'a love of beauty' be 'rooted in the life of the people.'"[2] Dietrichsen believed that, above all else, beauty and ornament should be logical and sensible: "What is sensible, it is true, is also the most beautiful . . . anyone can see that it is senseless, and thus ugly, to have a relief on the seat of a chair. A design for a chair like this would not reveal truth, either. A true chair is a chair that fulfills the function of a chair, namely that it be an object on which to sit."[3]

The Arts and Crafts and the Art Nouveau movements in the Nordic countries were both responses to this call for an interest in nationalism as well as craftsmanship-based social design countering the industrial trends of the day. But, like elsewhere, the movements, somewhat elitist in actual execution, were relatively short-lived. While the interpretations of the quotation above by proponents of twentieth-century Functionalism may have been different, they are both based in the idea that the function of an object should dictate its form and ornament (or lack of ornament) and that a well-designed object can have a positive social effect.

The cabinetmaking craft forms a rich tradition within Denmark. This tradition provided the basis of Denmark's Modernist pioneers in twentieth-century design: in short, it was the framework of the elitist but critical cabinetmaker's industry guild and the more populist Farmers Co-op, the appreciation for the beauty of wood, and the love of the refined yet understated aesthetic of classic English designs that would prove critical to the future development of the movement.

Swedish Traditions:
A Love of Lightwoods, Optimism, and Social Harmony

When we think of Scandinavian furniture as historically employing lighter, blonde woods and expressive fabrics, it is mainly Swedish furniture of which we are

thinking. Located to the north of Denmark, Sweden is largely composed of forests and lakes. The cabinetmaking tradition grew out of local country towns and villages where trees like birch, spruce, oak, pine, and beech were all indigenous. As did the Danes, the Swedes in the eighteenth and nineteenth centuries copied foreign styles, ultimately giving them a lightness and simplicity that the northern climate and long, dark winters required for spiritual survival. From the Gustavian period (1771–1792) to Biedermeier (1830–1850) to English-influenced Revivalism in the late nineteenth century, the Swedes continued to follow continental trends. Around the middle of the nineteenth century, Swedish design took a more populist and socialist approach with the abolition of the restricted membership Furniture Guilds. In 1846, the Swedish Society for Industrial Design (Svenskform) was founded with the operational goal of bringing social change through design. This concern for social harmony and well-being continued and became a hallmark of Swedish design in the twentieth century.

Swedish daybed in expressive contemporary fabric evoking the era. Kerstin Horlin-Holmquist daybed of upholstery and beech, 1960. Manufactured by Nordiska Kompaniet.

1917–1945:
Germinations of the Boom

The period of and between World Wars I and II can be seen in retrospect as the phoenix out of which the post-World War II growth period was formed. It was during this period that the key social and design constructs were formed in the advent of Modernism and Danish Modern in particular. The combination of social democratic values taking root in Denmark as well as the resuscitation of the cabinetmaking tradition through government, education, and industry would prove critical to the development of Danish Modern design.

In the early part of the twentieth century, a growing social democratic movement was afoot in Denmark and much of Scandinavia. Seeking to reform capitalism in order to eradicate perceived injustices, the movement had strong socialist tendencies and swept the Social Democratic Party into power in 1924; they remained there for the next seventy-seven years. The party's goals of social change and social responsibility were reflected in the design community: the party believed that good design and social progress were interrelated. Up until this time, the Danish furniture industry was in apparent decline and was once again primarily involved with copying furniture styles that were popular in Europe. In addition, there was a great deal of cheap factory-made furniture being imported, appealing to the masses. Conditions were seemingly ripe for the development of a new generation of designers and cabinetmakers to reinvigorate the industry. The story starts to unfold in 1917, around the same time of the Bauhaus/de Stijl movements, when Kaare Klint, a young man of twenty-five, began studying the interrelationship of people and furniture. Klint would later be credited with the birth of Danish Modern, the principles forming the foundation of inexpensive standardized production, and the revitalization of a cabinetmaking tradition in Denmark. However, like earlier attempts to revitalize the traditions of craft, the movement to reestablish the hegemony of the traditional cabinetmaker would prove only fleetingly successful.

Mahogany Swedish
Bar Cabinet, 1930s.
Manufactured by
Nordiska Kompaniet.

Kaare Klint: Father of Danish Modern

"To a certain extent, our endeavors coincide with those abroad, in particular with ones in Germany (the Bauhaus), but we feel that they are working on a more primitive basis regarding the use as well as the working out. Apparently, they have jettisoned all traditions, starting from scratch. What is a chair it is asked, where and in what way is the construction influenced by pull and pressure, etc. It is a laudable way of procedure, but a troublesome one, because in all probability one will not get answers to all the questions.

In preference to what is modern, one loses one's view and precludes the best aid, namely to build on the experience gained through the centuries. All the problems are not new, and several of them have been solved before. These new movements all over the world are, however, useful: it is no longer fashionable to surround oneself with antiques. A real interest in modern cabinetmaking has appeared and we welcome it sincerely."[4]

Facing: Interior shot with Kaare Klint chairs and sofa. Kaare Klint, easy chair #4488 of mahogany with rosewood inlay and cane, 1932. Manufactured by Rudolf Rasmussen.

PH series of hanging, wall, and table lamps later produced in 1927 with Louis Poulsen. These lamps, with modifications, were a phenomenal success and are still in production today. Henningsen was one of the few true Functionalists in the Bauhaus/de Stijl mold of designers believing in the power of production to bring good design to the masses.

Updated hanging version of the classic light designed in the 1920s, currently in production. Poul Henningsen design, 1958. Manufactured by Louis Poulsen.

Swedish Contemporary Decorative Arts at the Met (1927)

One of the earliest initiatives in developing broad public awareness of Scandinavian design in the U.S. was the Swedish Contemporary Decorative Arts exhibition that opened at the Metropolitan Museum of Art in New York in 1927. The exhibition featured over eighty different examples of ceramics, textiles, glass, and furniture. It was a huge success, attracting around fifty-five thousand visitors, and was instrumental in underscoring the quality of Swedish design.

Annual Exhibition of the Danish Cabinetmakers' Guild (1927–1966)

In 1927, the Danish Cabinetmakers' Guild founded an annual exhibition in Copenhagen to foster innovation in furniture design, stimulate the public's awareness, and revivify the demand for good furniture. It was partially conceived as a response to competition from Germany that was in danger of subsuming the crafts-based industry of the smaller Scandinavian country. Architects and designers were eager to work with cabinetmakers to create and show designs complementing the new styles of architecture being developed at the time. Cabinetmakers A. J. Iversen and Otto Meyer were the first to exhibit the designs of young architects like Kaj Gottlob. Soon more architects joined ranks and, in 1933, an annual competition for the design of new types of furniture was established and took place in advance of the guild's annual exhibition. Each winning design was produced by a cabinetmaker in the guild, often leading to longtime partnerships between the architects and cabinetmakers. A few examples of these partnerships include A. J. Iversen with Ole Wanscher, Erhard Rasmussen with Borge Mogensen, Johannes Hansen with Hans Wegner, and Rudolph Rasmussen with Kaare Klint.

Otto Schulz faux leather and birch wood cabinet, Sweden, 1944. Manufactured by Otto Schulz.

Brazilian rosewood desk by Jorgen Gammelgaard for cabinetmaker C. B. Hansens, 1957. Presented at the Annual Copenhagen Cabinetmakers' Guild Exhibition, where it won a silver medal.

employed expensive material and hand finishing. Indeed, much of what the Bauhaus designed later had to be adapted to accommodate industrial processes.

"The chair is a very difficult object. Everyone who has ever tried to make one knows that. There are endless possibilities and many problems—the chair has to be light, it has to be strong, it has to be comfortable. It is almost easier to build a skyscraper than a chair." — *Ludwig Mies van der Rohe*

Of course, not all of the designs of the Bauhaus architects had such a clear historical basis, but the Barcelona Chair is an iconic piece representing the movement. Klint's incremental and evolutionary philosophy of design, with its Scandinavian sensibility and Danish warmth, seems to have been addressing the same issues even if the mode d'emploi was different. Both had a profound impact on an entire generation of designers to come.

Stockholm Exhibition and the Arrival of Modernism in Scandinavia (1930)

The harbinger of Modernism in Scandinavia is widely accepted as being the Stockholm Exhibition of 1930, a show organized by Swedish architect Gunnar Asplund, which drew over four million people from around the region—a significant portion of the population at the time. The exhibition was the first with a completely modern bias, offering standardized and mass-produced items designed to meet the day's utilitarian and social needs. It was also a fitting symbol for political currents of Swedish social democracy. But Functionalism in its most extreme forms did not reach great numbers of the population, and domestic furniture in particular retained the traditional warmth of wood and cabinetmaking orientation while at the same time being influenced by a clean modernist form and focus on

Facing: Mies van der Rohe's renowned Barcelona Chair and table with vase by Danish ceramicist Axel Salto.

An example of a Kay Bojesen rocking horse in beechwood, 1936, presented at the Permanent Exhibition of Danish Arts and Crafts. Produced by Rosendahl.

function. Critics claimed that Swedish Modernism reflected traditional "national" virtues, rooted in Lutheranism and the age-old struggle against the harsh climate. Swedish Modernism was highly regarded elsewhere, especially in Britain, for its humanism and its distinctly local character.

Permanent Exhibition of Danish Arts and Crafts (1931)

Founded in 1931 by silversmith Kay Bojesen, director of Holmegaards Glasvaerk, and Christian Grauballe, the Permanent Exhibition of Danish Arts and Crafts in Copenhagen was developed as another means for designers of the decorative arts to exhibit and sell their designs. Inclusion in the showroom was juried, and participation was considered an honor for both the designer and the cabinetmaker. In the 1950s, the twenty-thousand-square-foot exhibition space became a stopping point for Danes and the international community as well. The exhibition was closed in 1988.

U.S. World Fairs: Chicago (1933) and New York (1939), When Swedish Grace or Swedish Modern Became the Rage

Scandinavians from all four countries participated in both world fairs, reaching almost fifty million visitors in Chicago and about forty-five million in New York. These were enormous events by today's standards, more akin to large television audiences than exhibitions, and they illustrate the impact such an event could have on the culture at the time. Finnish architect Alvar Aalto designed the Finnish pavilions, where some of his bentwood designs were present and were critically acclaimed. But it was also at the New York Fair where the term "Swedish Modern" came into usage. With regards to furniture, the style in Sweden was marked by simplicity, utility, and good quality, with a traditional warmth reflected in its Nordic form of functionalism. Carl Malmsten, Bruno Mathsson, and Austrian-born Josef Frank are the names that stand out in furniture design during this period.

Carl Malmsten is most famous for his unique handmade pieces influenced by the Swedish Gustavian and "rural rococo" style but with a modern, simplified elegance and function. He countered the extreme Functionalism of the continent,

believing in the value of traditional craftsmanship in the spirit of Kaare Klint. Similar to Klint, Malmsten founded several schools and was important as an educator and mentor. His furniture was well made, durable, and functional but exhibited a neoclassicism and less restrained expressiveness more typical of the Swedes than the Danes. (See example on page 140.)

In the 1930s, Bruno Mathsson began his research into the functions of sitting and lying down, creating new furniture forms from these studies. His experiments with bent and laminated birch, combined with his studies of function and comfort, have resulted in many classics, several of which are still in production today. In some ways, Mathsson was the Swedish equivalent of Klint, but his designs were lighter, more organic, and less influenced by historical archetypes. His famous Eva chair was designed in 1934. (See page 159 for an example of Mathsson's work.)

Josef Frank, who immigrated to Sweden in 1934, is the third light of the era. His Viennese roots, influenced by Adolf Loos and Josef Hoffmann, are fused with a Swedish-Anglo style that ultimately is all his own. Sold to this day by Svenskt Tenn in Stockholm, his works are pure poetry, employing traditional joinery and simple, beautiful woods with an apparent mix of Austro-Swedish classicisms.

Facing: Contemporary American interior with Swedish easy chair of ebonized birch, 1920s.

Josef Frank mahogany with rosewood top desk for Svenskt Tenn, 1960.

Years through World War II

Between the two world wars, the Danish furniture industry grew fairly quickly in response to the increased interest in nationally produced furniture as well as the increased urban population. There was a need for well-designed, smaller scale furniture, and the Danish furniture market grew with it.

Although they were not as directly involved in World War II as their neighbors on the Continent or in England, the Danish economy was impacted. While Sweden remained neutral, Denmark was occupied by Germany from 1940 to 1945. The Nazis were not able to scale the craftsmanship traditions of the furniture industry in Denmark to industrial needs of the war and they mostly left the Danes alone, a fortuitous development. Jewish architect/designers, such as Arne Jacobsen and Poul Henningsen, were impacted, however, and left the country for Sweden. Production slowed, along with the economy and the scarcity of quality materials like mahogany, and did not regain its full strength until the late 1940s.

Upscale production continues in Denmark despite the war. Ole Wanscher rosewood and leather armchair, 1940. Manufactured by A. J. Iversen.

Ole Wanscher mahogany and velvet buttonback sofa, 1944. Manufactured by A. J. Iversen.

1946–1967: World War II Ends and the Boom Begins

"Let's not get dizzy from success. The [increase in] exports is rather due to the fact that the Nordic taste suits a social stratum that is able to buy abroad, and they do not buy because of our blue eyes, but mainly because it is fashionable and they are snobs. Our democratic style has become comme il faut . . . but without a certain element of the fashionable, one cannot push valuable things." — *Poul Henningsen*[6]

Postwar economies in Europe emerged slowly from under the rubble of war with help from the American-led Marshall Plan, a farsighted effort to ensure the long-term stability and alliance of the European continent with the United States. What resulted, of course, is one of the greatest periods of creativity, growth, and prosperity in human history. During this period, the theories of Kaare Klint and the Functionalists in Europe and America were put to the test—could they effect social change through the democratization of design? The Danes and Nordic countries were well positioned to take advantage of this opportunity. Having been only marginally impacted by the ravages of two world wars, they could quickly scale their enterprises to cater to the increasing demand. Furthermore, with a tradition of craftsmanship, the investment was minimal—labor was in fact cheaper than machinery and raw materials during the postwar years, playing to the Danes' strengths. If the 1940s became the decade of Swedish Modern, the 1950s and 1960s belonged most squarely with the Danes. The collaboration between the designers/architects and the cabinetmakers would ensure that when the Danish furniture factories took up modern lines of production in the 1950s, the designers' background in working with craftsmen would impart knowledge of how a piece

Unique cabinet designed by Ole Wanscher for the 1946 Annual Cabinetmaker's Exhibition. Solid Cuban mahogany cabinet with carved reliefs, 1946. Manufactured by A. J. Iversen.

Exhibitions and Prizes during the Postwar Period

The postwar period was, of course, when the Scandinavians' design acclaim reached its apex. Interest and support for design was at a peak in Europe and the U.S., and the success of the Danes in influencing the new developing style and winning awards for their work during this period reinforced their image as the great arbiters of design and led to the great commercial success that followed.

Lunning Prize Established (1951–1970)

Frederik Lunning, the Danish owner of the Georg Jensen store in New York, along with members of the various decorative arts associations and guilds in Scandinavia, felt that it was an important marketing tool to establish an international identity and reputation for good design and craftsmanship abroad. The goal of the Lunning Prize was to stimulate creativity and quality in design and to develop awareness and the sale of these products in the Nordic countries and the U.S. The prize was awarded to two designers each year from 1951–1970. Hans Wegner was the first designer to win this award in 1951; later recipients in the furniture arts included Nanna Ditzel (1956), one of the few female furniture designers of the period, and Poul Kjaerholm (1958).

Milan Triennale (1951, 1954, 1957, 1960)

The Milan Triennale, founded in Italy in 1927, was the most important design exposition of its kind. Conceived as an Olympics of sorts for the applied arts, the expo featured awards given to the best designs by category. Grand Prix was the highest acclaim, followed by Gold, Silver, and Diplome d'Honneur. During the 1950s, the Scandinavians took a disproportionate number of the awards, winning the most prizes in 1951 and almost one-third of them in 1957. Danish furniture designers winning the award included Hans Wegner in 1951 and Ole Wanscher in 1960.

Good Design (1950–1955)

Good Design was a joint collaboration between Chicago's Merchandise Mart and the Museum of Modern Art in New York. Held annually, the exhibition was shown in both cities with the purpose of showcasing good design for the modern house-

Facing: An Ole Wanscher armchair and Nanna Ditzel desk give this study a warm and inviting feel. The desk, in Brazilian rosewood, has three drawers but was also available in a four-drawer version in oak, rosewood, and teak. Wanscher had several reiterations of this chair through his career. Ole Wanscher #2714 armchair, manufactured by A. J. Iversen, 1961. Nanna Ditzel desk, circa 1950. Manufactured by Søren Willadsen.

Period style. Ole Wanscher easy chair with English influence, upholstered with leather and Brazilian rosewood legs, 1959. Manufactured by A. J. Iversen.

hold for wholesalers and the public alike. The combination of curatorship by a premier museum and commercial support gave the everyday objects presented an unprecedented importance in the eyes of the consumer. While the focus was not uniquely Nordic, Finn Juhl was asked to design the first exhibition in 1951 because of his relationship with the promoter and MoMA curator, Edgar Kaufmann, Jr. Many Scandinavian designs were displayed. Borge Mogensen and Ole Wanscher, whose rocking chair by France and Son was on display in 1952, were among those furniture designers included over the years. Most of the items could be purchased concurrently or shortly thereafter at local stores. Examples were acquired for MoMA from each exhibition.

Design in Scandinavia (U.S. Tour 1954–1957)

Design in Scandinavia, an exhibition of enormous breadth and reach, began a three-year tour of twenty-two American and Canadian cities. The exhibition, which commenced in New York at the Brooklyn Museum, included all of the major arts and crafts associations and manufacturers in Norway, Sweden, Denmark, and Finland. Selected by a panel of twelve Scandinavians, three from each country, the exhibition featured seven hundred utilitarian objects for the home that were often available for purchase at local department stores. Furniture included designs by Hans Wegner (e.g. Round Chair, 1949, and Y-chair, 1950) and Borge Mogensen.

The Arts of Denmark (1960)

In 1960, the Metropolitan Museum of Art hosted another exhibition on Scandinavian design, this time reflecting the arts of Denmark and designed by Finn Juhl. While the Danes would have preferred an exhibit on modern wares, the museum wanted a more historical context fitting with the aims of the institution. Entitled "The Arts of Denmark: Viking to Modern," the show was sponsored by the Danish Society of Arts and Crafts and Industrial Design. The goal of the exhibit, as stated by then Prime Minister of Denmark Viggo Kampmann, was "to show our country in proper perspective . . . to give the world, in this case the United States, a full and genuine impression of Danish mentality, Danish ability,

Presented at the Arts of Denmark Exhibition in the U.S. Hans Wegner FH 4283 Chinese Chair shown in Brazilian rosewood, 1943. Manufactured by Fritz Hansen/P. P. Mobler. Made in rosewood, mahogany, walnut, cherry, or ash, the piece was recently reissued.

and Danish uniqueness."[8] An article from the *New York Times* declared that the "spare 'Danish Modern,' a revolutionary style of furnishings that made its appearance in the Nineteen Twenties, is the star of the long awaited show . . . Most visitors will feel immediately at home in the huge contemporary section, although certain aspects may be new to them."[9] As the article indicates, by 1960 the average consumer was increasingly aware and eager to incorporate Scandinavian design into his or her home. Furniture by Kaare Klint (sideboard, 1930s), Hans Wegner (Windsor Chair, 1947), Borge Mogensen (Hunting Chair, 1950), Finn Juhl (Sofa Bench, 1948), Ole Wanscher (folding stool, 1959), Arne Jacobsen (Egg Chair, 1958), Poul Kjaerholm, Mogens Koch, Jacob Kjaer, and many other designers were exhibited.

The opening was attended by the King and Queen of Denmark, and the exhibition was a major success, with over eighty thousand visitors. The show later traveled to Chicago (where it was presented at the Art Institute of Chicago), Washington D.C., and San Francisco.

The exhibitions and shows discussed previously were among many in the United States and abroad and contributed to the surge of interest in Scandinavian design by the public. Other notable shows included Forme Scandinaves held at the Louvre in Paris (1958), Creative Craft in Denmark Today held at the Cooper-Hewitt (1962), Two Centuries of Danish Design designed by Finn Juhl at London's Victoria and Albert Museum (1968), and Contemporary Finnish Design, a show curated by the Smithsonian that began a two-year tour of the United States in 1970.

1950-1960: Boom, Boom, Boom

The 1950s were a decade of great economic expansion in Western Europe and the United States and can be considered the decade of Scandinavian Modern. This was a period when many of the great designs were acclaimed successes, projects were commissioned, major exhibitions were staged, and, as discussed earlier, the Danish and Nordic designers seemed to sweep most of the prestigious awards for good design. Between 1950 and 1954, Danish exports to the U.S. increased almost five-fold. While food items such as canned ham and blue cheese were still the largest dollar earners, furniture and other arts and crafts played an important role. About 50 percent of all Danish furniture produced in Denmark during this period was exported to the United States. Other major markets included Sweden, Germany, and the United Kingdom.

Fueled by the strength of the dollar and the growing economy in the United States, Americans made their way through Scandinavia in large numbers while doing what came to be called the "Grand Tour" of Europe in the 1950s and 1960s. A review by Betty Pepis, the style editor of the *New York Times*, of the Permanent Exhibition in the summer of 1951 stated that it was mainly the province of the cabinetmakers and their more reserved and understated English styles rather than the more avant-garde designers that the mid-century was making famous. Kaare

Chair shown in the Permanent Exhibition in Stockholm 1951. Designed by Ib Kofoed-Larsen, teak and fabric chair, 1950. Manufactured by Christensen and Larsen.

Klint's Barcelona chair was among the chairs Pepis discovered, noting that the Danish furniture differed from American reproductions because they were adaptations to modern times. She also observed that copies of Klint's chairs were available all over Copenhagen—a situation that sounds awfully familiar to today's design world! Nevertheless, two hundred contributors representing twenty-six cabinetmakers and one factory were presented. Pepis followed up the article with a review of the Copenhagen Cabinetmaker's Exhibition in January 1951. While she noted an English-influenced desk by Jacob Kjaer, she focused on the more avant-garde work that was also being sold in the U.S. by designers such as Finn Juhl, Borge Mogensen (with his famous Hunting Chair), and Ib Kofoed-Larsen. The *New York Times* and many other U.S. publications went on to write a large number of articles on Danish and Swedish Modern during the period.

During the postwar years, there was a unique collaboration between governments, museums, and merchants in promoting cultural understanding and trade among countries. Much of what was on display in exhibitions was also available in shops at the time (or would influence the distributors of Scandinavian design in the U.S. to wholesale the merchandise). While curious by today's standards, this generation apparently grasped the importance of the design they were creating and how new and different it was. In the 1950s there was a proliferation of stores carrying Nordic goods, starting in New York and eventually blanketing the United States. A partial listing is included here:

- Georg Jensen on Fifth Avenue (and later on Madison Avenue) was an empire unto its own, carrying a wide range of Scandinavian decorative arts including Jensen silver. With 20,000–25,000 square feet of retail space, the store could devote a whole floor to furniture. Many lines were presented, including Poul Kjaerholm's designs.

- George Tanier opened a shop on Madison Avenue where he showed Borge Mogensen's furniture for the first time in 1951. Hans Wegner and many others were also carried.

- John Stuart, of the shop We Moderns in New York, was to the trade only and sold lines by France and Son, whose designers included Finn Juhl, Ole Wanscher, and Soborg Furniture, which worked with Borge Mogensen.

- Selig NY sold Kofoed-Larsens designs by Christensen and Larsen.

- Bonnier NY sold Josef Frank's furniture for Svenskt Tenn.

- Abraham & Straus in Brooklyn and Pacific Overseas in San Francisco were among others that sold Scandinavian designs.

- Fritz Hansen's Arne Jacobsen and Hans Wegner designs and Baker's line of Finn Juhl were available at their representatives across America.

Much to the detriment of the specialty stores, by the early 1960s many of the major department stores had gotten into the act, including Bloomingdale's, Macy's, and Lord & Taylor.

Josef Frank sideboard in mahogany for Svenskt Tenn, Sweden, circa 1960.

Below: Kerstin Horlin-Holmquist upholstery and beech Paradise Sofa, Sweden 1960. Manufactured by Nordiska Kompaniet.

1967: End of an Era

"New, new, new, just for the sake of newness, for the sake of the sales' curve, in order to make people throw away the old things before they have served their time. Not so long ago we looked for a better form, now we only have to find a new one."

— *Poul Henningsen*[10]

A new era defined by late 1960s culture. This is an example of Verner Panton's use of color and style. Textile, circa 1970.

By the early 1960s, there was already discussion of the expendable consumer society that the postwar period was creating. Danish design had been knocked off first by other Danes and was now being copied by Americans sourcing cheap imports from factories in Asia. Good design became indistinguishable from the cheap imports in the eyes of the consumer, undermining the values of a generation and a movement. Pop art, polyester, and all of the synthetic derivatives of petrol were changing consumer demands and society even more radically than earlier waves of Modernism. Made-to-last was replaced with disposable everything.

With the changing times, the enormous success of Scandinavia and the social democratic pact it made with its people began to undermine itself. As a result of the expanding social welfare state, labor became more expensive than the production plant, and the Danish furniture industry could no longer compete effectively. The skills of a craft-oriented society were superfluous in the postmodern world where the machinery of mass-production and mass-marketing seemed unsuitable for small nation states rooted in traditional values and craft like those in Scandinavia. The Annual Exhibition of Cabinetmakers closed for the last time in 1966, marking the end of an era for Denmark and perhaps the world. A deep crisis in furniture design ensued in the 1970s, with the sole shining light being Danish pop-artist and designer Verner Panton. Whether Danish Modern was an aberration or simply part of the path of evolution, the world certainly benefited in a way befitting the ideals of the movement.

While the idea of Functionalism was particularly appealing to Scandinavian architects and designers, it was, for the most part, a traditional functionalism based upon historical models, traditional craftsmanship, and studies of modern needs. The younger designers like Juhl, Jacobsen, and Kjaerholm, who rejected elements of the Klint school's views, nevertheless benefited from the Danish cultural paradigms of quality, understatement, and timelessness, which were in one way or another incorporated into their own individual styles.

A resurgence of demand for Danish and Scandinavian design was observed as early as the 1980s with the Cooper-Hewitt National Design Museum's major retrospective *Scandinavian Modern Design 1880–1980*. Since that time, there have been waves of interest with strong demand beginning in the 1990s. For many, it is a style that feels both familiar and new at the same time. In a world where we are constantly looking for the next new thing. Danish Modern has quietly stood the test of time, weathering fad after fad in the design world. Its historical roots and the clean elegance of its lines have enabled the style to cross over into a new century, to be discovered by a new generation. The guiding principles of functional form, the beauty of natural materials, and the quality craftsmanship that the masters of Scandinavian design applied to the creation of furniture are as relevant today as they were in the mid-twentieth century.

Reminiscent of Mies van der Rohe's 1930 Barcelona chair, this chair was produced in 1970. Proof of a classic is that the cycle recommences. Preben Fabricius and Jorgen Kastholm leather one-seat sofa BO-561, which was extendable, 1970. Manufactured by Bo-Ex.

Global Infusions:
Why Danish Modern *Mixes* So Well

Through the brief survey of the history of Danish Modern, many historical influences on the designers have been suggested—Egyptian, Greek, Chinese, Shaker, English, and Spanish. Most of us can probably identify when something looks Chinese or looks English, but beyond that, we are lost as to the specific historical references to which the designer was referring and what the significance of that might be beyond a pure aesthetic fantasy. For that reason, it is fitting and within the context of understanding the story of Danish Modern to very briefly look at some of those individual influences and the designs they effected.

Egyptian Design:
Roots of All Modern Furniture Techniques

The Egyptians are the oldest recorded civilization with furniture; indeed, many of the principles of modern furniture-making date back to Egyptian times. A wealth of information exists, as the practice of placing various articles such as food, jewelry, leather goods, textiles, and furniture into the graves of high ranking or noble persons was a common practice in ancient Egypt and the arid climate of the region made it possible for many of these items to be preserved. Much of what has been unearthed dates from the tenth through the twentieth dynasties, roughly 2000–1100 BCE.[1] The extant examples of furniture combined with pictorial materials, such as relief sculpture and wall paintings, give us an unparalleled look into the Egyptian art of furniture making.

The Egyptians had a fully developed artisan culture based around several simple yet practical forms. These forms and craft traditions were passed down through generations of craftsmen. The forms that they used correspond to many modern furniture forms that we are familiar with, such as folding chairs, chairs with and without arms, stools, footstools, case goods such as chests and cabinets, and advanced basketry and wickerwork. Egyptian craftsmen used many techniques that are common today, such as mortise and tenon, dovetailing, veneering, inlay work, and making plywood. They used a wide variety of materials in the construction of furniture such as cedar and ebony. Many materials were imported due to the scarcity of sturdy and versatile woods in Egypt. The craftsmen in Egypt had a long tradition of passing forms from one generation to another—consequently, those forms changed little.

While we have examples of many types of furniture, perhaps the most common form of Egyptian furniture found is that of the chair or throne. According to Ole Wanscher in *The Art of Furniture*, "The chair is a dominating form in Egyptian furniture, also in the visual arts. Since earliest times it has been a symbol of honor recognized in most cultures, both ancient and modern."[2] The chairs developed during Egyptian times share a similar simple, practical form and reasonable scale, allowing them to be easily moved to provide formal seating in a

variety of situations and functions. The thrones of royalty are similar in their form to chairs used by ordinary citizens; typically they have a strong square sloping back with stretchers extending from the back of the seat, supporting the back. The seat was either flat or scooped and woven from leather or twisted rushes. Chairs dating from the twelfth to the eighteenth dynasties typically have legs that are carved into naturalistic representations of animal legs, such as those of a lion or an ox. The animal leg was not only a favored decorative motif but also originally had religious significance. In addition to the carving on the legs, decorative motifs also included carving on the back, inlay, bone buttons, and line inlay.[3]

Another form favored by Egyptian craftsmen was the folding stool. It was developed in Egypt around 2000–1500 BCE as a portable seat for military com-

Mogens Lassen folding Egyptian coffee table shown in Brazilian rosewood, 1940. Manufactured by A. J. Iversen (later R. Rasmussen). Made in rosewood, mahogany, cherry, teak, or ash, the piece is still in production.

manders.[4] Seen as a symbol of authority and easily portable with its simple and lightweight construction, the folding stool was used by both royalty and religious leaders. The design of the stool consists of two wooden frames that turn on a metal bolt and a leather seat that is stretched over the frame to provide not only a flexible seat but also the topside of a strong triangular construction.[5] Variations of this form appear in many later cultures, including Classical Greek up until the Renaissance. The folding stool continued to function as a symbol of authority and power, both politically and ecclesiastically.

The impact of the Egyptian folding stool and other historical Egyptian forms can clearly be seen in Scandinavian design. Many Scandinavian designers used this form as a basis for their design, from Kaare Klint to Ole Wanscher to Poul Kjaerholm (see page 63). Wanscher made the most direct link to Egyptian forms with his Egyptian Stool that was based on a stool in the Staatliche Museum collection in Berlin.[6] The stool is elegantly simple with its soft curves and minimal seat. Wanscher captured the essence of the stool and gave it a modern life.

Classical Greece:
A Shared Past

Classical Greece shared a similar tradition of craftsmanship with Egypt. Traditional forms were passed from generation to generation, each improving on the work of the previous generation. Unfortunately, the Greeks did not have the same burial traditions or arid climate suitable for preserving organic materials such as wood that the Egyptians had, and there are few extant examples of Greek furniture. However, we can develop a picture of the furniture forms and finishes produced in ancient Greece by studying reliefs, coins, vases, and sculpture combined with literary sources.

Greek carpenters had a broad range of skills that they implemented in the creation of an expansive range of furniture forms. We know from literary sources that they incorporated inlay of ebony and ivory, gold and silver mountings, carpet cushions, and animal skins. In addition, they were familiar with such techniques as steaming and bending wood. While some of their furniture bears a resemblance to Egyptian prototypes, the Greeks had a wider range of specialized tools and incorporated turned elements in their construction.

One of the more common furniture forms found in ancient Greece is the Klismos chair, which was in use from about the sixth century BCE until the early part of the Hellenistic period.[7] In his book, *The Art of Furniture: 5000 Years of Furniture and Interiors*, Ole Wanscher observes, "One of the most interesting forms is the type of armchair known as the Klismos, the characteristic features of which are the curved, receding back and the sweeping lines of the resilient legs."[8] Early Greek chairs, like Egyptian thrones, had straight backs and rigid seats. The Klismos chair demonstrates a departure from this tradition. Its form is characterized by a curved, receding back, and graceful, flaring saber legs that curve outwards to the front and rear. The pronounced curvature of the legs served not only an aesthetic function but also allowed the legs to act as springs so the chair would rest evenly on any surface, both indoors and outdoors. The height of the back varied from a higher back, which indicates a stiffer, more formal seating position, to a lower back, which allows for a more relaxed, slightly reclined position and also

Facing: From a Danish Modern collector's house, a Mid-Century Modern homage to Greek design. T. H. Robsjohns-Gibbings Klini lounge chair in mahogany, 1961. Produced by Sardi's of Athens, Greece. The Klismos-based form has been experimented with for centuries but was reinterpreted by many including the Danes in the twentieth century.

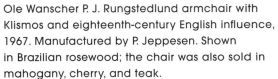

Ole Wanscher P. J. Rungstedlund armchair with Klismos and eighteenth-century English influence, 1967. Manufactured by P. Jeppesen. Shown in Brazilian rosewood; the chair was also sold in mahogany, cherry, and teak.

One of only six prototypes, this walnut chair of classical Greek Klismos influence was presented at the 1946 Annual Cabinetmakers' Exhibition in Copenhagen. Designed by architect J. Juul-Moller with the collaboration of cabinetmaker Knuud Juul-Hansen.

functions as an armrest. In Wanscher's opinion, it was the latter type that was "most in harmony with the easily moveable character of the Klismos form."[9] Wanscher's affinity for the Klismos chair can be seen in his Rungstedlund chair, whose form bears a strong resemblance to it. The chair's lightweight construction allowed it to be transported easily. Portability was essential in many early cultures, as furniture was costly and a family might only have a few pieces that would need to suit a variety of functions.

As previously mentioned, the folding stool was a common furniture form in Greece just as it was in ancient Egypt. Similarly, the Greek folding stool was associated with positions of power and was a symbol of dignity. It is commonly found in two forms, one made of several pairs of crossed staves placed close together and the other made of carved lion's legs facing inwards. These shapes were then adopted by the Etruscans and then later by the Romans. Throughout the centuries, the Greek folding stool retained its form and use as a symbol of power and dignity.

"They [the Klismos-inspired chairs] may seem to be almost at the edge of the abyss of decadence, but on the other hand, life is a dangerous game, and there is no lack of people who will be able to establish a natural balance."

—From the Annual Cabinetmakers' Exhibition catalogue
    for the booth entitled, "A Bachelor Makes Himself Comfortable"

Chinese Inspiration:
Ming Still Sings

Like Greek and Egyptian influences, Chinese furniture has proven to be a fruitful source of inspiration for many generations of European craftsmen. The Chinese influence is particularly evident in English furniture dating from as early as the late seventeenth century through the eighteenth century. Both the Queen Anne and Chippendale styles of furniture have elements that can be directly linked to Chinese furniture. Scandinavian designers were influenced directly by the study of Chinese furniture as well as later stylistic interpretations infused into English furniture. The connection should not be lost that Brazilian rosewood, used so extensively in Danish Modern furniture, was also the most likely and affordable proxy for the Chinese hardwood huanghuali.

China was the first nation outside of Europe to adopt "chair-level living" before the late nineteenth century.[10] Chairs did not become commonplace in Chinese society until about the tenth century.[11] Previously, people commonly sat on mats or on low platforms with armrests. While the earliest chairs appeared in the sixth century in a Buddhist context, people did not sit on chairs but rather knelt on the seat. During the Song Dynasty, it became customary to sit upright with the legs pendant. The change from kneeling to sitting in chairs brought with it a host of changes to other aspects of life in China. For example, new forms of furniture were developed or adapted, such as the higher-level table. Social and eating habits changed, and there were architectural changes to both the exterior and interior of the home.

In ancient China, there was a strict hierarchy in seating: who you were dictated where and on which kind of chair you sat. A high-ranking official might be given a high-back chair while those of a lower status might be given just a stool. Chairs were often draped with lavish textiles in order to indicate a person's rank or to create a ceremonial seat. Comfort was not the most important consideration in seating. The posture adopted in all but the most informal of situations was erect, with the feet perched on a footstool or the front stretcher of the chair.

Facing: Philippe Starck's Louis ghost chairs surround Ole Wanscher's Ming-inspired dining table for A. J. Iversen, which allows the simple beauty of the table to transpire. Brazilian rosewood was a proxy for the Chinese hardwood huanghuali used in earlier times. This table was also made in both rectangular and round coffee-table versions of various sizes.

One of the most recognizable Chinese chairs is the round back chair, or basket back chair, as it was referred to during the Song Dynasty. The back and armrests of this chair form a continuous line with outward curving hand rests. The hand rests are not only decorative but also served to hold textiles in place when the

This is one of many versions of dining chairs throughout the period with Chinese influence. Dining sets during the period usually matched. Ole Wanscher Ladder-back chairs, made in mahogany or rosewood. Manufactured by Illums Bolighus.

Ole Wanscher Ming chair, shown in walnut and occasionally found in rosewood, 1943. Manufactured by Fritz Hansen.

chair was draped for ceremonial use. In addition to ceremonial use, the chair was used in various places around the house and garden. Paintings tell us these chairs were often used in pairs or even sets of four, although there are very few sets found today. The round back chair was the inspiration for Hans Wegner's Chinese Chair, which was designed for Fritz Hansen in 1944 (see page 53). Wegner was intrigued by the round back chair because of the freedom in movement given to the sitter by the combined top rail and arms. He took the basic form of the chair and simplified it, eliminating the bottom stretchers and most of the traditional ornamentation. However, Wegner kept the distinctively shaped apron beneath the seat, an element that both strengthens the chair and provides a finishing element. He continued to return to the round back chair throughout his career, using its shape as the inspiration for several more pieces such as the iconic Wishbone Chair.

Another common chair form is the yokeback armchair, or official's hat chair, with four protruding ends. This chair featured a high yoked back with straight arms and an S-shaped splat (a flat piece of wood in the center of a chair back). This splat is similar to the splat found on the round back chair and was often decorated with a carved or inlaid motif. It is called the official's hat chair because the yoke is said to resemble the winged hat that was part of Ming officials' formal dress. Because of its high back, the chair is associated with a position of power and would have often been draped with textiles to create a ceremonial seat. The slightly upturned ends of the yoke helped to keep those textiles in place. The southern official's hat, or continuous yokeback, armchair is a similar shape; however, the ends of the top rail and arms do not protrude, producing a smooth, linear flow. In addition, the back splat is C-shaped rather than S-shaped. This form was popular among scholars, and these chairs are often pictured in studios or studies. An armchair designed in 1943 by Ole Wanscher for Fritz Hansen echoes the form of the southern official's hat chair with its smooth rounded form and yoked back. In place of the central splat, he used a double splat to add visual interest. Wanscher did not limit his use of Chinese motifs to chairs; many of his tables echo these same motifs.

Chests during the period frequently had Chinese influence. This one by Borge Mogensen was a modular sideboard/ bookshelf unit available in rosewood, teak, and oak. The influence of Professor Kaare Klint on his pupil is evident but the chest is executed in a lighter, more modern way than in Klint's classic sideboard. Shown here in teak, the piece features a corresponding drawer unit and available bookshelves, making the use modular.

English Furniture

Much like the language, English furniture has roots in many classicisms and lends itself to many interiors. Indeed, eighteenth-century and early-nineteenth-century English furniture is an interesting mix of vernacular furniture styles indigenous to England combined with styles from the Continent and from many of the cultures already discussed, such as Egyptian and Chinese. The Danes borrowed from all of these traditions but most extensively from the English. Some of the less successful examples seem like outright copies, while others go beyond glorious in their interpretations of the style.

The association between Denmark and England can be attributed to their proximity as well as a long historical relationship. For more than one thousand years, the Danes and the English have been linked, beginning with Canute, King of both Denmark and England, who reconciled the two warring countries and united them into one kingdom. The relationship has generally remained strong ever since. The Danes have long demonstrated an interest in English furniture, dating back as far as the late eighteenth century, when an institution called the Det danske Mobelmagasin, or "The Danish Furniture Stores," was founded. The goal of the institution was to advise and educate Danish furniture makers. In addition to supplying them with wood, providing them a place to sell their work, and lending money, the institution gave craftsmen designs on which to base their work. Many of these designs were supplied by "cabinet-makers and architects who had studied in England and who were exponents of that English combination of comfort and dignified simplicity."[12] This interest continued into the twentieth century with two exhibitions, held in 1928 and 1932. These exhibitions illustrate the interest by design professionals in English furniture designs and help to explain the strong English influence on design in Denmark. The first exhibition, *Engelske Mobler fra det 18. Aarhundre I dansk Eje*, held in 1928 at the Museum of Decorative Art in Copenhagen, exhibited eighteenth-century English furniture from Danish collections both public and private. The exhibition showed examples of such vernacular furniture styles as the Windsor chair alongside pieces of the Chippendale and Hepplewhite styles. The second notable exhibition, *Britisk*

Facing: These chairs, modern with English sensibilities, form a comfortable conversation area in this study. Ole Wanscher's Easy chairs in leather and mahogany, 1938. Manufactured by A. J. Iversen.

Ole Wanscher's Chippendale-inspired Wavy chair in mahogany with leather seat, circa 1946. Manufactured by F. Hansen.

Brugskunst, or British Applied Art, was held in 1932, again at the Museum of Decorative Arts in Copenhagen. Steen Eiler Rasmussen, who had lived in Britain and had taught at the Architectural Association in London, organized the exhibition.[13] It featured a selection of furniture as well as everyday objects. Its intent was to illustrate the restraint in ornament and craftsmanship that was associated with English furniture and objects.

The Chippendale style was named after Thomas Chippendale, who published a furniture design book in 1754 called *The Gentleman and Cabinetmaker's Directory*. Its public success led to several editions published in short succession. The third and final edition, published in 1762, featured over two hundred designs for tables, chairs, and more specialized forms of furniture such as basin stands and fire screens. One of the styles that Chippendale drew upon for his furniture designs was Chinese. One can see the influence in his dining chairs. Many of his chairs feature a delicately carved yoke back not unlike the Chinese official's hat chair (which, as previously discussed, was also used by the Danish).

Another furniture style that Scandinavian designers drew upon was the neoclassical style. George Hepplewhite and Thomas Sheraton popularized this furniture style in the late eighteenth century. Hepplewhite, an obscure cabinetmaker in London, collected three hundred furniture designs that were published in 1788, two years after his death, by his wife, Alice. The volume was titled

One of many desks from the period with English inspiration. Ole Wanscher three-drawer desk, shown in Brazilian rosewood, circa 1960. Manufactured by A. J. Iversen.

The Cabinet-Maker and Upholsterer's Guide, and it was intended to promote "English taste and workmanship"[14] to neighboring countries. The name Hepplewhite is often used to describe a very narrow and particular type of design, specifically a chair with a square tapered leg and an oval or shield back. However, his book also featured designs similar to those found in the book by Thomas Sheraton, *The Cabinetmaker and Upholsterer's Drawing Book*. The designs found within Sheraton's book are primarily of classical origin, such as the Klismos chair. (See Ole Wanscher's Rungstedlund chair on page 68.)

Cabinetmaker Frits Henningsen's Chesterfield-inspired sofa in mahogany and leather, circa 1930s.

A prime example of the English melding of vernacular styles and furniture traditions is the Windsor chair. Produced primarily by rural craftsmen, this chair was made in a wide range of styles and sizes. The basic form of the chair is relatively simple. The back is generally either a horizontal, comb, or bow back fashioned from a single piece of wood such as yew or ash. Interestingly, the back struts of the chair extend from the back of the seat in a similar fashion to chairs made in ancient Egypt. The seat is created out of a solid piece of wood, most commonly elm, carved into the shape of a saddle seat. The legs are generally turned on a lathe and placed at an angle. While the basic form may have been simple, a great deal of skill was needed to create a chair that was sturdy, lightweight, and easily moveable.

This style of chair was hugely popular in both England and in North America, and there were a great many regional variations of the chair. However, while there may have been stylistic variations, the principles that guided the basic form of the chair remained the same. Scandinavian designers displayed a great deal of interest in the Windsor chair and began to reproduce and export them to England: "Between 1949 and 1952 several thousand archetypically British Windsor chairs fitted comfortably into British homes with few people noticing that they came from Denmark."[15] Both Ole Wanscher and Borge Mogensen designed Windsor chairs for production. Indeed, many Scandinavian designers looked towards vernacular English furniture and the quality of a high standard of craftsmanship associated with that furniture for inspiration.

Restraint in ornament and a focus on craftsmanship were indeed banners taken up by the proponents of the so-called "English Style." Most notably, this group included Kaare Klint, cabinetmaker Jacob Kjaer, Ole Wanscher, Frits Henningsen, and Mogens Koch. Jacob Kjaer is quoted as saying that "eighteenth-century English furniture has often inspired our craftsmen who seem to have felt instinctively attracted to the sound elegance and skills of the old English masters."[16] All of these men were members of the Cabinetmakers' Guild and exhibited their designs at the guild's exhibitions. Unlike some who simply reproduced English furniture styles, these designers used historic styles as a source of inspiration and adapted those furniture types for modern use, believing that "these 'timeless types' were furniture forms that had been made through generations and were thus seen to have proved the practicality of their design."[17] Essentially, they felt that one did not have to reinvent the wheel when designing furniture that was both beautiful and functional. This idea was central to the functionalist movement in Scandinavia.

One of many versions of the classic English Windsor chair produced by the Danes in the twentieth century, this one in elm is by cabinet-maker and designer Frits Henningsen.

Shaker Traditions: Modern?

The story goes that Kaare Klint was the first to unwittingly be introduced to Shaker furniture when he saw a ladder-back rocking chair and ordered measured drawings of the chair to be used as one of his famous classroom aids in analyzing historical chairs. But only in 1937, when Edward Deming and Faith Andrews's influential book *Shaker Furniture: The Craftsmanship of an American Communal Sect* became available in Denmark, did the Danes learn the Shaker origin of the rockers that had inspired them so profoundly. This later influenced Borge Mogensen, who went on to produce his Shaker-inspired line for F. D. B. Mobler, as well as Hans Wegner, Ole Wanscher, and others. When Mogensen's and Wegner's furniture began to be imported to the United States in the 1950s, the circle was complete.

The original founders of the Shakers came from England (hence the connections with vernacular English furniture as well), where they were often persecuted and imprisoned for their beliefs. In order to escape this persecution, they fled England for the United States in 1774, settling near Albany, New York. They quickly converted groups of people in nearby New Lebanon, New York, and in Hancock, Massachusetts. The Shaker communities quickly grew, and by 1794 they had established eleven communities in New England. They eventually settled in Ohio and Kentucky as well.

The Shaker way of life was focused on simple and utilitarian communal living, with equality between the races and sexes. Simplicity could be found in all aspects of life, from dress to food to furniture. In the 1790s, Joseph Meacham, a prominent leader of the Shakers, warned that "all work done or things made in the Church for their own use ought to be faithfully and well done, but plain and without superfluity."[18] Up until 1800, there was little to distinguish the furniture produced in these communities as distinctly Shaker. However, newly converted craftsmen brought with them knowledge of the standard form of the outside world. This sparked a period of experimentation and the development of a style that is characterized as distinctly Shaker. Long before Louis Sullivan and Frank Lloyd Wright (the great Chicago architects) or the German Bauhaus, led by Walter Gropius, began developing their principles. Shaker furniture embodied the modern spirit of form following function. The Shakers believed that "beauty rests on utility. That which has in itself the highest use possesses the greatest beauty."[19] The early Shakers worked hard to make a living and had little time to spend on decorative details and frills. They held the idea that useless ornamentation encouraged pride or vanity. In addition, they were greatly concerned with cleanliness and therefore eliminated ornamentation that would attract dust and be difficult to clean. Upholstered chairs, sofas, daybeds, and canopied beds were rejected out of this concern. Drawers and cupboards were built into walls and furniture and under seats to provide places where items could be stored away—a place for everything and everything in its place.

Clean and simple lines with warm woods and traditional craftsmanship characterize Shaker furniture, which is perhaps one of the reasons that it resonated

Facing: Ole Wanscher's PJ311 Colonial Chair with Japanese Edo period plate in the background, 1959. Showing Shaker influence in design, this chair also came in the typical Shaker caned seat (see page 92).

Borge Mogensen School Chair #121 in beech and teak (also produced in oak), 1952. Manufactured by Soborg Mobelfabrik or Munch Mobler.

with modern Scandinavian designers. Early Shaker furniture was often painted or finished with a thin red, yellow, or blue stain. Later pieces which were used as inspiration for the Danes would be simply varnished or stained. While Shaker teaching discouraged ornamentation, their furniture was not completely void of ornament. Craftsmen incorporated the natural beauty of special woods such as curly maple as well as turned posts and finials into their designs. Chairs were the most common item of Shaker furniture. Craftsmen made a wide variety of chairs that addressed the individual purpose for which the chair was created. For example, as chairs gradually replaced the benches commonly used around dining tables, chairs with low backs were created so that they could be pushed under the table.

The Shaker community placed a great deal of emphasis on the quality of craftsmanship. The idea of craftsmanship was linked with the idea of morality and purity. Members were encouraged to "do all your work as though you had a thousand years to live on earth and as you would if you knew you must die tomorrow."[20] Craftsmanship was encouraged at every level of production, from the simplest spoon to an elder's desk; they differed, however, from another group of Americans, the Amish, as Shakers embraced modern technology as progress and left us many inventions, including the circular saw.

Danish Modern: Classic Mixing and Matching

After centuries of use, it is fascinating how fresh and modern some of the forms that inspired Danish Modern still seem to us today. The traditional job of the cabinetmaker is, of course, to construct the furniture so that it never wears out; many of those techniques, as we have seen, have been around for centuries. And the goal of any great designer is to develop a timeless piece of furniture that seems forever fresh and vital.

With its infusions of the best of classical forms dating from antiquity through eighteenth-century design, the Danes were able to develop a style that paid homage to the Greeks, Egyptians, Chinese, English, Spanish, and Shakers while incorporating the Scandinavian ethos and remaining true to modern needs and uses. It is this sort of early globalization of design that permits the melding of the period's furniture so gracefully into traditional and contemporary decors.

Indeed, the term "modern classics" applies to many of the Scandinavian designs from the period included in this book. The color of the fabric or the leather may change, and we may prefer a high gloss polish or matte finish on the wood, but those forms that continue to engage us through time become classics. Styles will certainly come and go, but classic pieces never really fade away entirely. In that way, Danish Modern has already stood the test of time.

Hans Wegner AT 305 three-drawer desk, 1955. Manufactured by Andreas Tuck, P. P. Mobler. Shown in oak. Also available in ash, mahogany, and cherry.

Cabinetmakers' Guild:
Selected Designer *and* Cabinetmaker Briefs (1927–1966)

The emergence of the Cabinetmakers' Guild exhibitions in the late 1920s was critical to the eventual success of Danish Modern as it brought design out in a very public forum for debate and review. In addition, it encouraged a healthy amount of competition among the architects, cabinetmakers, and furniture manufacturers. The periodical *Kritisk Review*, founded by Poul Henningsen in the 1920s (and quoted throughout this book), was one of the forums of debate during the period.

Previous overleaf:
Mogens Koch wingback
chair in mahogany and
leather, designed 1936,
produced 1964 by Interna
and later cabinetmaker
R. Rasmussen.

The passion in which design was discussed and the intellectual framework around it is remarkable by American standards—although it certainly became acrimonious at times! There is also no doubt it was a big and profitable business for the Danes, but many at the center of it were also trying to change the world in a deep and profound way. If the architect/designer's role was to bring new ideas, the cabinetmaker's was to determine feasibility and execute. It was the interplay between these two forces that was really dynamic. To elicit commercially viable designs rather than intellectual fantasies, the architect/designer generally worked on a royalty basis, earning around 2 percent of retail price or 5 percent of wholesale (although exceptions existed). This section gives a brief overview of some of the key designers and cabinetmakers of the period; in all, there were 75 cabinetmakers and 233 designers who participated over the forty-year period (which is beyond the scope of this book). There is a certain bias towards those who have already been recognized internationally (e.g. Finn Juhl), were instrumental in the development of the period (e.g. Kaare Klint), who were prolific in terms of number of designs (e.g. Ole Wanscher), or who made important contributions (e.g. Frits Henningsen). These are some of the key designers and cabinetmakers that have resurfaced on the American and international markets of late.

The Tired Man Easy Chair
by Flemming Lassen,
upholstered in new
leather. A. J. Iversen 1936.
You can see the resem-
blance to Arne
Jacobsen's Egg Chair
(page 106).

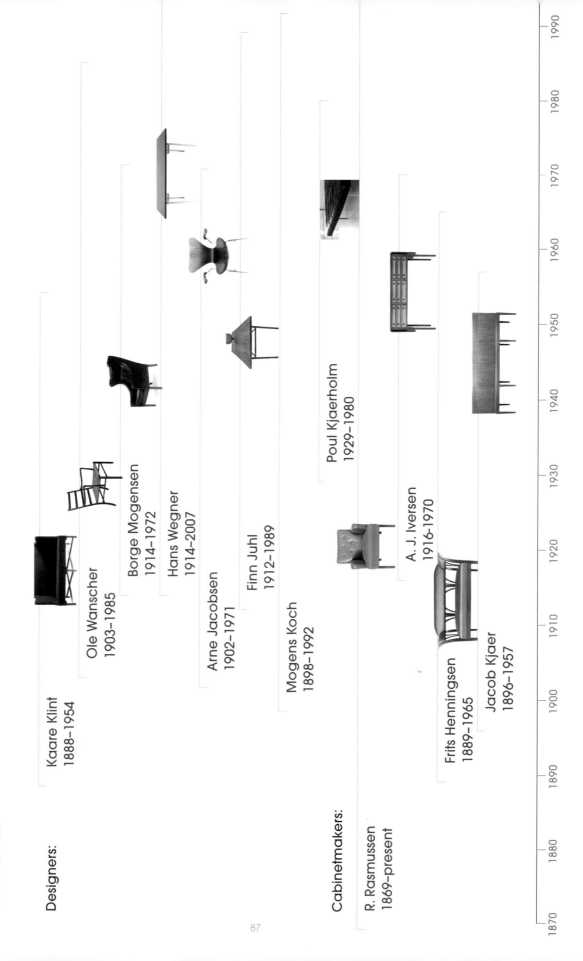

Timeline of selected designers
and cabinetmakers with
important pieces of Danish
Modern furniture.

Designers:

Kaare Klint
1888–1954

Ole Wanscher
1903–1985

Borge Mogensen
1914–1972

Hans Wegner
1914–2007

Arne Jacobsen
1902–1971

Finn Juhl
1912–1989

Mogens Koch
1898–1992

Poul Kjaerholm
1929–1980

Cabinetmakers:

R. Rasmussen
1869–present

Frits Henningsen
1889–1965

Jacob Kjaer
1896–1957

A. J. Iversen
1916–1970

1870   1880   1890   1900   1910   1920   1930   1940   1950   1960   1970   1980   1990

Kaare Klint
1888–1954

"It is of no use to design furniture; it cannot be designed."

— *Kaare Klint*, Mobilia Magazine, *No. 56, 1960*

Kaare Klint RR#4396 Easy Chair of mahogany and leather, 1930. Manufactured by cabinetmaker Rudolf Rasmussen.

Honors

Eckersberg Medal, 1928

Grand Prix, World Expositions in Barcelona, 1929

Brussels, 1935; Bissen Prize, 1938

Royal Designer of Industry, London, 1949

C. F. Hansen Medal, 1954

Key Designs

Barcelona or Red Chair

Safari Chair

Folding Stool

Faaborg Chair

Sideboard

RR#118 Loveseat

RR#396 Chair

Years Exhibited at Cabinetmakers' Guild Exhibition

1930–31, 1933, 1937–38, 1941, 1946, 1948, 1952–54

(1960, 1962, 1964, 1966 posthumously)

Background

Kaare Klint was the son of prominent Danish architect Peder Vilhelm Jensen-Klint and served as an apprentice architect for him. His father instilled in him the importance of studying historical precedence. Klint originally wanted to become a painter but found himself drawn into architecture and, eventually, furniture design. From 1911 to 1912, Klint worked with architect Kai Nielsen and then from 1914 to 1917 with architect Carl Petersen. He established his own

Facing: Close-up of Kaare Klint's Barcelona chairs with Chippendale influence. Kaare Klint Barcelona or Red Chair of mahogany and ox hide, 1927. Manufactured by Rudolf Rasmussen. Pupil Borge Mogensen's Asian-inspired modular chest #232 designed in the 1940s for F. D. B. Mobler, C. M. Madsen is displayed with an Axel Salto stoneware piece for Royal Copenhagen from 1949. Danish ceramicist Inger Thing is represented in the background under a painting by contemporary Swiss artist Alex Hanimann.

Kaare Klint oval dining table shown in Cuban mahogany, circa 1930. Manufactured by cabinetmaker Rudolf Rasmussen.

design firm in 1920 and began working with cabinetmakers Rudolph Rasmussen, Fritz Hansen, and Otto Meyer. He was a perfectionist and only designed thirty pieces during his life. A story has been told, presumably in jest, of a young engaged couple who ordered a double bed from him and received it just in time for their silver wedding anniversary!

Klint was appointed the first Chair of the Furniture Department at the School of Architectural Design, the Royal Danish Academy of Fine Arts, in 1924, where he had the opportunity to teach younger designers such as Ole Wanscher and Borge Mogensen. He was a charismatic and rigorous teacher who would often enlist his students in support for his research on anthropomorphic proportions and modern-day storage issues. In 1944, Klint also became professor of architecture at the Royal Academy.

Design Philosophy

While teaching at the academy, Klint developed a system of standard dimensions based on the proportions of classic furniture types, the human body, and the storage needs of everyday objects. He believed that by studying these dimensions, he could create furniture that was better suited for modern needs. Klint embraced historical styles not for their aesthetic value but for their functional qualities.[1] He thought the functionalist approach of ignoring historical prototypes was akin to reinventing the wheel, and he encouraged his students to study historic furniture in order to gain a better understanding of proportion and function. Klint's teaching at the academy laid the groundwork for a generation of designers, such as Ole Wanscher and Borge Mogensen, who would incorporate his principles and theories into their own designs.

In addition to designing furniture, in 1944 Klint designed the Fruit Lamp made of folded paper for Le Klint, a lighting company his father had established.

Cabinetmakers/Manufacturers

Rudolf Rasmussen

Fritz Hansen

Otto Meyer

"Klint's strength lies not only in the fact that he has undertaken this strictly scientific analysis of the fundamentals of furniture design. He is also a sensitive artist with a perfect knowledge of the techniques of cabinetmaking and with an unflagging energy and doggedness when it comes to finding the right solution based on empirical data . . . I wonder if it is possible to find more beautiful handmade furniture anywhere, so natural, so precise and correct down to the last splinter."

— *Willy Hansen, 1930*, Danish Furniture 1927–1936, *pg. 88*

Kaare Klint RR#4118 T (two-seater) of mahogany and leather, 1937. Manufactured by Rudolf Rasmussen.

Ole Wanscher PJ 149 Colonial chair of Brazilian rosewood (also available in mahogany and oak), 1949. Manufactured by P. Jeppesen. This chair has been recently reissued.

Ole Wanscher
1903–1985

Honors

Milan Triennale Grand Prix, 1960

Copenhagen Cabinetmakers' Annual Prize, 1960

Key Designs

Egyptian Folding Stool

T-Chair

Colonial Chair PJ149

Rungstedlund Set

Years Exhibited at Cabinetmakers' Guild Exhibition

1931, 1933–1934, 1938, 1940, 1942–1944, 1946–1954, 1956–1966

Background

Ole Wanscher was the son of an art historian and studied under Kaare Klint at the Royal Academy of Fine Arts. He traveled abroad extensively studying historical and vernacular furniture from many different cultures. In 1927, he helped to

"It could be argued that it is extravagant to use rosewood,

which nowadays has bad associations for many people,

but like silver, good craftsmanship will still find a buyer."

— *Ole Wanscher, 1932*[2]

Facing: Ole Wanscher Round back chair with arms with contemporary art in the background, shown with rosewood finish and horsehair. Manufactured by P. Jeppesen.

establish the Copenhagen Cabinetmakers' Guild Exhibitions that were held annually until 1966 and was a member of the jury for the annual design awards given by the guild. Wanscher wrote many articles and several books on the subject of historical furniture, including *Furniture Types* (1932), *Outline History of Furniture* (1941), *English Furniture circa 1680–1800 (1944)*, and *History of the Art of Furniture (1946–1956)*. In 1955, he succeeded Kaare Klint as professor of

Ole Wanscher Wingback chair #L-2872 upholstered, with rosewood legs, circa 1960. Manufactured by A. J. Iversen.

the Department of Furniture Design at the Royal Academy, where he taught until 1973. Personality-wise, he was considered aloof and rather elitist, unlike the charismatic Klint. While he was incredibly prolific and had successful relationships with several cabinetmakers, he is considered largely in the shadow of Klint and his contemporaries. One can only surmise that was because his poetic designs, while technically beyond compare with any of his peers, were the most deeply rooted in the bourgeois traditions of historical forms. While his designs were conceived and executed for some of the best cabinetmakers in Europe at the time, such as A. J. Iversen, he was nevertheless one of the first to actually apply his designs to broader production and had relationships with France & Son, Fritz Hansen, and P. Jeppesen.

"Wanscher can make something out of nothing, or at least it sometimes seems that way when you see his furniture. He has been particularly successful in the field of chairs. His pieces are like cars or radios that undergo slight, sometimes imperceptible changes every year."

— *M. K. Michaelsen, 1934*[3]

One of many versions of an Ole Wanscher armchair in mahogany and leather for A. J. Iversen, circa 1962.

Design Philosophy

Wanscher's designs were heavily infused with the historic classicisms about which he studied and wrote. Reflecting classical Chinese, Egyptian, and English furniture of the eighteenth century, his pieces also occasionally referenced the Shaker style. Wanscher used traditional materials such as mahogany and rosewood, with acute attention to details and joinery that are unmatched. While more traditional than some of his contemporaries, his designs reflect the combination of historical influences and the beautiful, clean lines that became associated with modern Danish furniture design. Throughout his years displaying in the Copenhagen

"Ole Wanscher's method of working is quite literally unique, and he never ceases to fascinate us with his ability to make his chairs new and original by adapting well-known models."

— *Erik Lassen, 1962*[+]

Cabinetmakers' Guild Exhibition, Wanscher resisted the pressure to exhibit new designs simply to attract attention. Instead, he focused on perfecting each design and allowed them to evolve organically, despite criticism that his designs were too traditional and static. Wanscher's designs, created in partnership with A. J. Iversen, demonstrate not only a high level of attention to detail but also attention to the execution of design that engages not only the eye but the human form as well.

Ole Wanscher custom silver chest of Brazilian rosewood. Manufactured by A. J. Iversen.

"As with his predecessor, the English influence is obvious. While Klint must have been preoccupied with other things, Wanscher has pursued the study of sitting postures with a thoroughness that pushes even the most vociferous functionalists into the background."

— *Klaus Meedom, 1963*[5]

Ole Wanscher Regency loveseat (also available in three-seat version), made with rosewood or mahogany legs, 1960. Manufactured by A. J. Iversen.

"If one owns a chair made by Wanscher, it will be an experience every day—perhaps for hundreds of years, because that is how long it will last. One senses the man behind the chair and the value of man-made work. A machine will make perfect products, but they have no soul."

— *Politiken: Sven Erik Moller, 1958*[6]

A. J. Iversen is long since defunct, but some of Wanscher's designs have recently been reintroduced by P. P. Mobler.

Cabinetmakers/Manufacturers

A. J. Iversen

P. Jeppesen

R. Rasmussen

Fritz Hansen

France & Son

Thorald Madsen

Chest on legs, Brazilian rosewood. Example made by P. Jeppesen. This chest coordinates with the Rungstedlund dining room set. A similar chest and table were also made by cabinetmaker A. J. Iversen.

"This is furniture which has not just been designed for the moment." — *Arkitelcten: E Zeuther Nielsen*

Borge Mogensen
1914–1972

Honors

Eckersberg Medal, 1950

Copenhagen Cabinetmakers' Guild Annual Prize, 1958

Danish Furniture Prize, 1971

C. F. Hansen Medal, 1972

Royal Designer of Industry, London, 1972

Key Designs

Spanish Chair

2213/4 Sofas Hunting Chair

J-39 Shaker Chair (This is the most well-known chair in Denmark, created because too much round wood was bought by the cabinetmaker and Mogensen was asked to find a use for it!)

Years Exhibited at Cabinetmakers' Guild Exhibition

1939–1951, 1953–1956, 1958–1963

Borge Mogensen Conference chair #3245, produced in rosewood, wenge, teak, and leather, 1962. Manufactured by Virums, and Fredericia.

Background

Borge Mogensen began his education at the School of Arts and Crafts in Copenhagen from 1936–1938. He then continued his studies under Kaare Klint at the Royal Academy of Fine Arts from 1938–1941 and served as Klint's assistant at the Royal Academy of Fine Arts between 1945 and 1947. In 1940, he introduced a line of furniture designed specifically for children called "Hansen's Attic" and then later "Peter's Bedroom." From 1942–1950, he served as the head of the furniture department of the Association of Danish Cooperative Wholesale Societies developing a line of furniture to be priced reasonably for the general public. In 1950, he opened his own design firm where he designed for Soborg Mobelfabrik, Fredericia Furniture, and Karl Andersson & Sons. In addition, he collaborated with Grethe Meyer (cabinet storage systems), Lis Ahlmann (textiles for C. Olesen), and Hans Wegner (furniture for Johannes Hansen).

Facing: Borge Mogensen's sideboard in Brazilian rosewood designed in 1957–1958 and produced by P. Lauritzen and Sons. Artwork by Charles Arnoldi and lamp by Poul Henningsen for Louis Poulsen designed in 1927.

Borge Mogensen Hunting chair (dining chair version) #3237 in oak and leather, 1951 and 1964 by Erhard Rasmussen, Fredericia.

Design Philosophy

Mogensen's designs often reflect Klint's interest in the storage solutions for everyday objects in modern apartments. Over the years, he designed many different series of cabinets that were modular in form and could be used for different purposes. He employed what he referred to as the "workshop method." He endeavored "by means of unremitting, objective labor, on the task of clarifying, sorting and classifying all the practical and constructional demands imposed by any given problem."[8] Like Klint, historical models inspired many of Mogensen's designs and the functional beauty of Shaker and Chinese furniture captivated his imagination. He also based several designs on Spanish forms. Perhaps of all the designers of this period, Mogensen was the most concerned with creating furniture that was able to meet the needs of the average practical family. He designed furniture for every room of the home, taking into consideration the person who would be using the furniture. Mogensen was a prolific designer and often exhibited his work with different cabinetmakers during the same year at the Cabinetmakers' Guild Exhibition. That many of Mogensen's pieces are still produced by Fredericia to this day is a testament to their enduring quality and design sensibility.

Cabinetmakers/ Manufacturers

Fredericia

Erhard Rasmussen

P. Lauritsen

Jacob Kjaer

I. Christiansen

Johannes Hansen

F. D. B. Mobler

C. M. Madsen

Borge Mogensen Wingback easy chair #2331, produced in mahogany and leather, 1963. Manufactured by Fredericia.

Borge Mogensen A234
Modular drawer cabinet
shown in teak, 1940s.
Manufactured by F. D. B.
Mobler.

"Kaare Klint's pupils have inherited his keen interest in storage furniture, and just as they have upheld his principles regarding the standardization of measurements, many of them have found it natural to continue the development of his aesthetic ideals. In this concise storage unit, Mogensen has transferred Kaare Klint's clear principles of division into simple box forms from the sphere of distinguished cabinetmaking to an industrial product of high technical quality. The doors of the sideboard are hinged in two sections, a construction which reduces to a minimum the amount of free space necessary in front." (See photo on page 98.) — *Arne Karlsen*⁹

Hans Wegner CH 318 dining table in rosewood (also in round), 1960. Andreas Tuck, manufacturer or, later, Carl Hansen. Originally in rosewood, teak, wenge, oak, or beech, it has been reissued in a variety of finishes.

Hans Wegner
1914–2007

Honors

Lunning Prize, 1951; Milan Triennial: Grand Prix, 1951, Diplome d'Honneur and gold medal, 1954, silver medal, 1957; Eckersberg Medal, 1956; Copenhagen Cabinetmakers' Guild, Annual Prize, 1959; Honorary Royal Designer of Industry, Royal Society of Arts, London, 1959; Citation of Merit, Pratt Institute of Decorators (for Furniture Design), 1961; International Design Award, 1961; Prince Eugen Medal, 1961; Copenhagen Cabinetmakers' Guild Annual Prize and Anniversary Grant, 1965; International Design Award, American Institute of Interior Designers, New York, 1967; Citation of Merit, American Institute of Interior Designers, 1968; Diploma di Collaborazione Triennial di Milano, 1973; Danish Furniture Prize, 1980; C. F. Hansen medal, 1982; Danish Design Council Annual Prize, 1987

"I have always wanted to make unexceptional things of an exceptionally high quality that ordinary people could afford." — *Hans Wegner*[10]

Key Designs
Chinese chair
Y chair/Wishbone chair
Shell chair, Peacock chair
Ox chair
Papa Bear chair

Years Exhibited at Cabinetmakers' Guild Exhibition
1938–39, 1941–66

Background

Hans Wegner was the son of a master cobbler and grew up with an appreciation of craftsmanship and materials. He apprenticed in H. F. Stahlberg's carpentry

Facing: Hans Wegner's EJ 100 Ox chair and stool #46 designed in 1960 and produced by Johannes Hansen and later, Erik Jorgensen. This was Wegner's favorite chair and sat in the middle of his living room. It is still in production.

workshop and continued to work for Stahlberg for another three years until he began his military service. While still in the military, Wegner took joinery classes at the Technical College in Copenhagen. As part of his studies, he was sent to the Copenhagen Museum of Decorative Arts to measure historical furniture on display. He attended the Copenhagen Cabinetmakers' Guild Exhibition, seeing works by Kaare Klint, Ole Wanscher, and Mogens Voltelen that would eventually influence his style. He decided to pursue a career as a designer and enrolled in the School of Arts and Crafts in 1936, where Orla Molgaard Nielsen was his teacher. In 1938, he found work with architects Erik Moller and Flemming Lassen, who were designing the Århus Town Hall with Arne Jacobsen. Wegner's job was to design furniture for the Hall. He worked for the pair of architects until 1943 when he established his own design office in Århus. From 1940, Wegner worked with furniture maker Johannes Hansen and designed many pieces of furniture for him, including the Round chair (1949), otherwise known simply as The Chair. The Chair became famous because it was used during the U.S. presidential debates in 1961 between John F. Kennedy and Richard Nixon.

Design Philosophy

Like many of his contemporaries, Wegner's design philosophy is grounded in the tradition of cabinetmaking and historical models. Many of his designs, such as the Peacock chair and the Chinese chair, have clear historic roots. In Wegner's own

Hans Wegner AT304 X-base table with drop leaves, available in teak or oak, circa 1950. Manufactured by Andreas Tuck.

"When you buy a piece of furniture, turn it upside down.
If the bottom is in order, the
whole piece probably is—
and vice versa."

— *Hans Wegner*[11]

Hans Wegner CH 29
X-back side chair,
available in teak,
oak, or beech, 1952.
Manufactured by
Carl Hansen.

words, his designs are the result of a "continuous process of purification . . . simplification, to cut down to the simplest possible elements of four legs, a seat and combined top rail and arm rest." His philosophy can be seen in The Chair, perhaps the most emblematic of Wegner's designs. He revisited this form over and over again in his designs.

Cabinetmakers/Manufacturers

Johannes Hansen

Andreas Tuck

Getama, A. P. Stolen

Carl Hansen and Son

Ry Mobler

Fritz Hansen

P. P. Mobler.

Today, much of Wegner's furniture continues to be produced by Carl Hansen & Son, Fredericia, and Fritz Hansen.

Arne Jacobsen
1902–1971

Honors

Silver Medal, World Exposition, Paris, 1925; The Academy's Small Gold Medal, 1926; Eckersberg Medal, 1936; Honorary Prize, Biennial, San Paolo, 1954; C. F. Hansen Medal, 1955; Grand Prize and Silver Medal, Milan Trienniale, 1957; Grand Prix International d'Architecture, 1962; ID Prize, 1967 and 1969; Plaque, Akademie der Künste, Hamburg, 1969; Gold Medal, Academie D'Architecture de France, 1971; Ph.D. Honoris Causus, Oxford University, 1966

Key Designs

The Egg chair

The Ant chair 1951 (over 4 million sold)

The Swan chair

Series 7 chair

Years Exhibited at Cabinetmakers' Guild Exhibition

1932

Facing: Arne Jacobsen's Egg chair designed for the SAS Royal Hotel in Denmark in 1958 in original leather. Produced by Fritz Hansen. Currently in production.

"It is exceptional that one chair—or one type of chair has been in fashion for over forty years. I can only compare Arne Jacobsen's [Ant] chairs with the Thonet chairs, which seem to have a similar quality. They fit in and may be used for any purpose and one cannot date them, the Thonet chair has been produced for 150 years, and I believe that this will also be the case with the Ant."

— *B. Henriksen*[12]

Arne Jacobsen FH#3207
Series 7 chair, 1955.
Available in rosewood,
teak, beech, or laminate.
Manufactured by Fritz
Hansen.

Background

Though he dreamed of becoming a painter while growing up. Arne Jacobsen was first and foremost an architect. Initially, he trained as a mason at the School of Applied Arts, Copenhagen, and graduated in 1924. He went on to study architecture at the Royal Academy of Fine Arts, Copenhagen, and after graduating from there in 1927, he worked for two years as an assistant in the City Architect's Office in Copenhagen. In 1929, he teamed up with Flemming Lassen to design the House of the Future—a circular home that featured a helicopter landing pad on the roof—for the building and housing exhibition held by Copenhagen's Academic Architect's Association. Jacobsen designed several pieces of furniture made of tubular metal for the home, his first foray into furniture design. In 1930, he set up his own architecture and interior design firm in Hellerup. One of the first commissions he received was for the Rothenburg House in Ordrup. The largest of early projects he completed was the beachside apartment blocks at Bellavista with adjoining Bellevue restaurant and theater complex. This large-scale project was completed in several stages from 1932 to 1935. In 1936, Jacobsen collaborated with Erik Moller to create a winning design for competition of the Århus Town Hall. This project was a contrast of modern architectural forms combined with soft organic forms that draw in the visitor. During the war years, Jacobsen and his wife fled to Sweden to avoid Nazi persecution as a Jew. Jacobsen was honored in 1956 with a position as professor emeritus at the Royal Academy of Fine Arts in Copenhagen, a position he held until 1965. During his term as a professor, Jacobsen continued to be a successful architect and furniture designer; in 1956, he began work on perhaps his best-known project, the SAS Royal Hotel and Air Terminal in Copenhagen. Jacobsen designed every detail that went into this project, from textiles to cutlery to light fittings to furniture. It was for this project that he designed his well-known Egg and Swan Chairs, which employed technology enabling lightweight fiberglass shells. The result of his hard work was a completely conceived modern hotel that, while minimal and constrained, had a humanist quality which permeates all of Jacobsen's work. While the hotel has

"To me, he cannot be characterized as a functionalist. Rather he was an architect with an incredible ability to simplify things. In that sense he continues a Danish or Scandinavian tradition."

— *Professor Henning Larsen*[13]

changed over the decades since its completion in 1960, one room, 606, has been preserved with its original furniture and color scheme. In addition to his long-standing relationship with Fritz Hansen, from 1955 to 1960 he worked with Louis Poulsen to design a line of lighting fixtures. He also created the Cylinda line of metalware for Stelton in 1967; cutlery for A. Michelsen; textiles for August

Millech, Graucob Textilen, and C. Olsen; and a line of cylindrical bathroom fittings for I. P. Lunds. In 1960, he designed the architectural scheme for St. Catherine's College in Oxford. He conceived of this project, which was similar to the SAS Hotel, as a total design, designing not just the architecture but the interiors and furniture as well. It is in this project, as well as the SAS Royal Hotel and Air Terminal, that we are able to see the full range of Jacobsen's talent and ability to create his vision in any media.

Design Philosophy

Jacobsen's architecture and furniture designs are perhaps the most modern of his Danish contemporaries. He conceived of his architectural projects as a whole and often designed furniture, textiles, lighting, and even cutlery for specific projects. He was a very hard worker, more expressive than theoretical in nature. Rather than being conceptual and intellectual in the design process, Jacobsen seemed to come up with designs intuitively. While his work displays little of the historical influences that his contemporaries drew upon for inspiration, the organic forms he chose are distinctly Scandinavian in clean line and modest understatement. His designs pushed the envelope of both technology and design. The development of the Ant chair was one such design. While other designers such as Charles and Ray Eames in the United States had worked with the process of double-curved, steam-bent plywood, Jacobsen worked with manufacturer Fritz Hansen to take the technology one step further by reducing the back and the seat of the Ant chair into one piece, a feat that was accomplished only by narrowing the back, giving it its characteristic shape. The Ant was designed with three legs—Jacobsen refused to allow it to be produced with four. The four-legged version was therefore put into production posthumously. Jacobsen was perhaps the most successful in creating furniture that could be and was produced for a mass market.

Cabinetmakers/Manufacturers

Fritz Hansen

Louis Poulsen

Stelton

Arne Jacobsen Modular Bookcase originally for hanging, wenge, circa 1950s. Manufactured by Fritz Hansen.

Finn Juhl
1912–1989

Honors

Milan Triennale 1954 and 1957 (five Gold Medals)

Eckersberg Medal 1947

Copenhagen Cabinetmakers' Guild prizes (fourteen awards)

Honorary Royal Designer for Industry (London)

1978. Knight of the Royal Order of Dannebrog. 1984

Key Designs

Pelican chair (1940)

45 Armchair or NV-45

Chieftain's chair 1949 (about eighty produced by Niels Vodder and
a similar version produced by Baker Furniture)

Egyptian chair. 1949

Bwana Easy chair. 1952

Years Exhibited at Cabinetmakers' Guild Exhibition

Twenty-four years, commencing in 1937, twenty-two of which were with Niels Vodder and two with Ludvig Pontippidan

Background

Finn Juhl was born in Copenhagen to a father who was a textile wholesaler representing British and Swiss textile companies. His mother died three days after his birth, leaving his father to raise him in a rather authoritarian household. Juhl studied at the Royal Danish Academy of Fine Arts in the Architecture School under Kay Fisker, an important and influential architect working in the international functionalist style of the period. However, he was self-taught when it came to furniture and cabinetmaking. He originally wanted to be an art historian, but his father would have nothing of it and Juhl compromised by enrolling in the Academy with the hidden agenda of studying art history at the same time. Inheriting a sum of money when he turned twenty-one, he set out on his own.

Finn Juhl Table bench, shown in rosewood and oxidized metal, 1953. Manufactured by Bovirke/Søren & Hansen.

Cabinetmakers/Manufacturers

Rudolf Rasmussen

Interna

Danish C. W. S., and N. C. Jensen Kjaer

Mogens Koch wingback chair in mahogany and leather, designed 1936, produced 1964 by Interna and later cabinet-maker R. Rasmussen.

"There was this shop in London which had in its window a shag-pipe 'The World's Best Pipe,' that was—and then this idiot comes along and asks to see their collection. No, they had 'The World's Best . . .' and then there was no need to offer something of lesser quality. What peace this offers. You can just walk into a shop and get the best. You would yourself, after many years of looking around, find the third best." — *Professor, Architect Mogens Koch* [15]

Poul Kjaerholm
1929–1980

Honors

Grand Prix. Milan Triennale, 1957 and 1960; Danish Society of Arts and Crafts, annual prize, 1957; Lunning Prize, 1958; Grand Prix and Gold Medal for Danish section. XII Triennale. Milan, 1960; Eckersberg Medal. 1961; Knud V. Engelhardt Memorial Grant. 1964; Danish Manufacturers' Prize for PK 27. 1971; 1971 ID prize for the PK 27; Danish Furniture Manufacturers' Prize for Louisiana Chair. 1977

Key Designs

Twenty designs, all of which are very similar in feel if not function
Some notable ones:

PK12 Tubular Steel Armchair

PK22 Lounge Chair

PK61 Coffee Table

PK80 Daybed/Bench

PK91 Folding Stool

Background

Poul Kjaerholm apprenticed as a joiner in Hjorring to Master Cabinetmaker Th. Gronbech from 1944–1948. In 1949, he enrolled in the Furniture Design Department in the School of Arts and Crafts in Copenhagen. During his studies there, Hans Wegner employed him part-time. After graduating in 1952, he was employed by Fritz Hansen and worked at their factory in Allerod. He returned to the school the following year to become an instructor and taught until 1956. His tenure overlapped his employment as an assistant teacher in the Department of Furniture Design at the Royal Danish Academy of Fine Arts, where he taught from 1955–1959. He was promoted to Associate Professor in the Department of Furniture and Spatial Art at the Royal Academy of Fine Arts in 1959 and served until 1973 when he became the supervisor of the Department of Design at the Academy. In 1976, he succeeded Ole Wanscher as Professor of Furniture Design and Spatial Art.

A. J. Iversen

Years of operation: 1916–1970

Years Exhibited at Cabinetmakers'
Guild Exhibition

1927–1966

Notable Designs

Tired Man Easy Chair

T-Chair

Egyptian Stool

Designers

A. J. Iversen, Ole Wanscher, Mogens Lassen,
Kaj Gottlob

Background

A. J. Iversen's simplified furniture may be seen as a
link to older Danish traditions of respect for historical
design while imparting Danish sensibility and refine-
ment. From the beginning of the Cabinetmakers'
Guild Exhibition, A. J. Iversen worked with architects
to produce crafted furniture that reflected the changing
lifestyle and architecture. Iversen was able to maintain
the tradition of Danish cabinetmaking while utilizing
the latest technology and was one of the few cabinetmakers who designed as well as executed his own furniture. He worked extensively with Ole Wanscher and
executed many of Wanscher's finest pieces, some of
which are found throughout this book.

Ole Wanscher Ming
round occasional table,
shown in Brazilian rose-
wood. Manufactured
by A. J. Iversen.

Facing: A collection of
Ole Wanscher rosewood
and mahogany furniture
including storage cabi-
net, chairs, and desk,
all designed in the
1950s and produced
by A. J. Iversen.

Easy chair with arms, in
leather and Cuban
mahogany, 1932.
Designed and produced
by Frits Henningsen.

Frits Henningsen
1889–1965

Years Exhibited at Cabinetmakers' Guild Exhibition
1927–1934, 1936

Key Designs
Rocking Chair (1930)
Easy Chair (1930)

Background
Little is currently known about the life of this designer and cabinetmaker, but he
was active in the Cabinetmakers' Guild Exhibition from 1927. His designs have
both elements of the traditional and organic style that characterizes early designs
of the period.

Writing desk shown in
Brazilian rosewood, 1950.
Designed and produced
by Frits Henningsen.

Facing: Frits Henningsen
armchair in Cuban
mahogany, circa 1930s,
shown with pieces of a
collection of American
Indian artifacts—eclecti-
cism at its finest.

Jacob Kjaer
1896–1957

Years Exhibited at Cabinetmakers' Guild Exhibition
1928–1956, 1958–1960

Key Designs
FN chair

Designers
Ole Wanscher, Borge Mogensen, Rigmor Andersen, Flemming Lassen,
O. Molgaard-Nielsen, Acton Bjorn, A. Bender Madsen, Aage Windeleff,
Tyge Hvass, Grete Jalk, Einer Larsen, B. Helweg-Moller, Carl H. Nimb,
Helge Holm, Preben Thorsen, Peter Hidt, N. C. Jesen Kjaer, Mogens Koch

Honors
Hand Work Medal, 1954

"As of yet, there are only a few cabinetmakers who are capable of
making their own designs, and consequently partnerships with
'outsiders' are not unusual. Among these, special mention should
be made of Jacob Kjaer and A. J. Iversen." — *Ole Wanscher, 1935*[21]

Sideboard in Cuban mahogany, 1954. Designed and produced by Jacob Kjaer.

"The English style is beautifully represented by Jacob Kjaer, who has a large stand with 'individual pieces of furniture' in Cuban mahogany, designed by himself, and with upholstered furniture designed by the architect Flemming Lassen." — *Ole Wanscher, 1935*[22]

Pair of easy chairs in mahogany, circa 1930s. Designed and produced by Jacob Kjaer.

Background

Jacob Kjaer was a furniture designer as well as a cabinetmaker in the tradition of Kaare Klint. His clean, graceful designs bear tribute to English style while clearly being modern in interpretation and attention to detail. He was active in developing the international profile of the Danish furniture industry and served as president of the Cabinetmakers' Guild Exhibition from 1952–1957 and of the Arts and Crafts Committee For Export from 1944–1957.

"Right by the entrance one immediately comes across Jacob Kjaer's stand with various pieces of furniture, designed by the architect Flemming Lassen and by himself—pure and clear in form, even his multi-purpose desk, a combined writing and sewing table . . ." — *Berlingske Tidende: Bouboule, 1935*[23]

This chapter illustrates a wide range of American interiors from all over the country, including spaces designed by young professionals starting out, interior designers' own abodes, abodes for young families and empty nesters, homes for single folks, and homes with wonderful collections built over many years. All of the interiors show how successfully these designs can mix with our modern lifestyle.

Without a doubt, there is a general affinity to the contemporary aesthetic in most of the interiors; however, the Danish Modern pieces here grace traditional homes as well as the ultra-modern, creating drama and interest. In addition to Danish Modern, you will see the incorporation of many eighteenth-century French and English pieces, Asian period classics, and twentieth-century icons from France, Italy, and the United States. In this way, traditional homes are given a punch of excitement and unexpectedness with the Scandinavian pieces, and the contemporary homes with a modern aesthetic have an added warmth, depth of texture, and awareness.

Maybe most notable is the degree to which the modern collector focuses on style over pedigree. There is simply no aversion to mingling fine wares with stylish pieces of lesser importance or even mass production, reflecting today's more relaxed lifestyles and the desire to maintain a home and not a museum. Individual style and passion trump conformity and purity of style—many interior designers can recount their clients' desires to do their own thing and break all the rules (whatever may be left of them, of course).

Most of the rooms presented do nevertheless favor neutral backdrops or warm earth tones with colorful accessories and art. This achieves a versatility in modern interiors that doesn't force individual rooms and objects to be "color coded" (think the ubiquitous green garden room of yesteryear). One of my own design rules is that an individual piece of furniture or art must be flexible; if it is only going to work in one specific room in one specific house, it probably is not a worthwhile investment. In modern America, we are transient and need flexible pieces that can work in many different rooms and many different interiors in different parts of the country. Sideboards, for example, should be useful in a dining room as serving and storage pieces, in a living or family room to add style and background under the increasingly present flat-screen television, grace a long hallway, or even act as storage space in a bedroom. In apparent confirmation of this, five of the seventeen households illustrated in this book had already moved before the book was published. Interestingly, not a peep has been heard from the people involved looking to dispose of those classic pieces they had acquired—in fact, quite the opposite has happened, attesting to their timelessness and versatility. One of my favorite sayings is "Furniture gets bored, like people, so one should move it around." If you do, your friends will think you redecorated and your interior will stay fresh and interesting. Change the paint color and you will really throw them.

All of the following homes fearlessly pursue their own varied interests in design and art with a mix of Danish Modern design. The success of this is generally assured by the understated yet refined nature of all the homes; the interiors presented are a combination of elegance with unpretentiousness that is suitable for entertaining, raising families, or just relaxing.

No book on Scandinavian design would be quite complete without some reference to IKEA. The molded beech chair in the distance, designed by Noboru Nakamaru, is a takeoff on the famous Bruno Mathsson chairs and the designs of Finn Alvar Aalto. Original idea, inspiration, or knockoff? It's hard to say, as the concept of the chair itself has been around for centuries.

The Genesis of a Collection
Chicago, Lakeview

A young professional family makes a fervent start at incorporating Danish Modern into a first home with a self-generated art collection. Serving as a backdrop for entertaining as well as for rearing young children, this minimal space is defined with a couple of select Danish pieces. An easy chair, ideal for getting a young child to transition from playtime to sleep, adds punch to the living room. The beautiful Danish rosewood table is flanked by family-oriented yet chic Louis ghost chairs. Add a tablecloth and the family eats without worries! True to my principle that pieces should incorporate easily into any interior, this young family has already integrated these pieces into a larger home and expanded their collection along with their family.

Philippe Starck's Louis ghost chairs flank Ole Wanscher's Ming-inspired Brazilian rosewood dining table for A. J. Iversen. The chairs, while inexpensive and practical, give a transparency to the magnificent grain of the rosewood table and the detailing and execution of this timeless Wanscher classic.

Mogens Lassen's Tired Man Easy Chair, designed in 1936 and produced by A. J. Iversen, is perfect for an exhausted Google client manager at the end of a long day. Finnish designer Anne Kyyro Quinn's contemporary pillow in felted wool rests on a vintage-style American sofa that is great for lounging or entertaining.

Kaare Klint's sofa #6092 by R. Rasmussen, designed in 1940, is the centerpiece of this fireside living area along with a pair of caned Klint Easy Chairs #4488, also by R. Rasmussen (design 1932), and Ole Wanscher's wavy back chair, circa 1946, by Fritz Hansen. Isamu Noguchi's 1955 coffee table by Knoll mixes gracefully with the Danish design, adding texture and vitality.

The Evolved Collection
Chicago, Gold Coast
Interior Design by Jack Andrews and Peter Shull

Elegant bliss describes this home in a Beaux Art Chicago masterpiece building overlooking Lincoln Park. The owners started collecting twentieth-century pieces in the mid-nineties and quickly discovered the wonders of mixing Nordic design as their eye and their scholarly approach dictated. The furniture collection focuses on those rare but magnificent works of design based upon classical models and forms. The couple have an innate, refined sense of style that allows them to mix and mingle pieces as they see fit, which evolves as the opportunity and desire arises. While passionate about Danish Modern, they are not slaves to the style and have thus created an unusual and intriguing interior based upon their own aesthetic and desire for comfort. The earth tones and smaller seating areas work in large rooms to create a greater sense of warmth and comfort. Varied and lush textures of fabrics are mixed with wood and metal to give depth to the look. Colors are subdued yet rich.

A set of Frits Henningsen dining chairs gracefully surrounds a contemporary table.

A chest designed circa 1920s by Carl Malmsten of Sweden is shown with a collection of Danish and other ceramics.

Frits Henningsen's highly sought-after and curvaceous wingback in original leather, designed circa 1939.

A Passionate Mix
Chicago, Lake Shore Drive

Designed by Swedish-born architect L. G. Hallberg and built by the Danish firm Jens Jensen and Son in 1916–1917, this apartment is located in a classic Beaux Art building on Chicago's famed Lake Shore Drive. A fusion of old and new, the space represents a search for what speaks to the soul. Evolved rather than planned, the home features a consistency of clean lines and classic forms with an Asian-inspired bias, no matter what the genre or period.

Here, as with the first two interiors, the couple goes with their own eyes, one pair more traditional and one more modern, woven together as great relationships must be. Multicultural backgrounds, international assignments, and transcontinental living arrangements somehow created a successful mix of Asian with English style, Louis XVI with contemporary Italian pieces, and all with Danish Modern. No rules exist except to find comfort, harmony, and tranquility while integrating family heirlooms, expatriate furnishings, and other souvenirs gathered along the road of life.

Facing: The entrance to this Beaux Art apartment features Ole Wanscher's table for Ilums Bolighus in Brazilian rosewood. Axel Salto's celadon vase for Royal Copenhagen, produced in 1949, sits on the table.

A pair of Ole Wanscher easy chairs rest gracefully in front of the Beaux Art fireplace with a contemporary Danish sculpture on the coffee table.

This Swedish neoclassical cabinet in golden flame birch and rosewood with ebonized details, circa 1920, resides underneath a collection of family portraits.

A Cuban mahogany three-drawer desk by Ole Wanscher, produced by A. J. Iversen, accompanies Art Deco chairs in the "office."

Facing: The living room is set off by a pair of Swedish neoclassical barrel-back chairs in birch, circa 1920, situated in a mostly traditional setting.

Urban Tranquility
Chicago, Gold Coast
Interior Design by Semel Snow Interior Design, Inc.

A respite from the busy world, this home in a beautiful prewar building overlooking Lake Michigan in Chicago manages to be at once cozy and a professional place of business. A combination home office/study in painted wood was created out of a former dining room to serve as the workspace while an adjoining area spacious enough to be used as a combination living/dining room serves for relaxing and entertaining. The home reflects a mingling of existing furnishings, found objects, family heirlooms, and Danish and Swedish designs. The Scandinavian pieces were specifically selected as they were able to fulfill the various design challenges of a small dwelling that needed to double as a home and work space. The scale of the pieces as well as their emphasis on form, function, and style graciously complements the rest of the beautiful but modest-size cooperative apartment. Many find Scandinavian design perfect for urban spaces for these very reasons.

Previous overleaf: Kaare Klint's Barcelona Chair #S4751 in horsehair by R. Rasmussen, designed in 1927, mixes gracefully with a vintage Italian dining table and contemporary art.

Ole Wanscher's armchair #A2714 designed in 1961 and produced by A. J. Iversen with Wanscher's coffee table by Fritz Hansen circa 1940s.

Facing: Ole Wanscher's ladder-back chairs in mahogany and horsehair by A. J. Iversen, designed 1942.

The Real Thing: Danish Hygge
Chicago, Lincoln Park

Kaj Bojesen's rocking horse designed in 1936.

"Hygge" is a Danish word that is almost untranslatable but loosely means coziness, comfort, warmth, and ambience all at once. This pre-war apartment, owned by a Danish-American family in Chicago's Lincoln Park, reflects that spirit with a collection of Scandinavian furniture and art. With generous public entertaining areas and adjoining family living quarters, a kind of casual elegance is achieved. A sense of light is achieved with neutral walls and warm-toned mahogany furniture. The collection of Danish furniture reflects the need for home yet feels completely natural in its newly found environment, mixed with American furnishings new and old. This bicultural family has thus found a kind of natural harmony within the two cultures and traditions.

The collector's dream dining room, with a collection of Ole Wanscher's pieces in mahogany designed for Copenhagen's main design store, Ilums Bolighus, in the mid-twentieth century.

A collection of Danish pieces by Ole Wanscher, Ilums Wikkelsoe, and Swedish designer Bruno Mathsson graces the living room. In the foreground is a three-seat modular sofa by Ilums Wikkelsoe designed in 1960 and produced by C. F. Christensen. A pair of Ole Wanscher armchairs, PJ312 in rosewood, and coffee table produced by P. Jeppesen and designed circa 1950–1960 completes the set. In the right corner is a nod to Swedish style with Bruno Mathsson's classic Pernilla lounge chair in beech designed in 1934.

The master suite leads into a dressing room with Mogensen chests.

A pair of Borge Mogensen modular Chinese-inspired chests with drawers occupies the walk-in closet. The pieces were designed in the 1940s and produced by F. D. B. Mobler/C. M. Madsen.

Facing: The daughter's cozy hideaway features a Kaare Klint #4118 two-seat sofa in black wool designed in 1937 and produced by R. Rasmussen.

Following overleaf: Arne Jacobsen #3107 chairs for Fritz Hansen in Brazilian rosewood accompany American Paul Evans's sofa circa 1970.

And Now for the City Loft

A regenerated table is surrounded by Arne Jacobsen's Armchair #3107 in molded rosewood (designed in 1955) for Fritz Hansen and Kindt-Larsens's dining chairs for Thorald Madsen in original black leather (designed in 1960).

Borge Mogensen's Easy Chair #2207 of English influence designed in 1963 for Fredericia fits comfortably in an otherwise contemporary living room of French and Italian pieces. This chair was also produced in loveseat and sofa versions. The sofa version graced Danish embassies around the world.

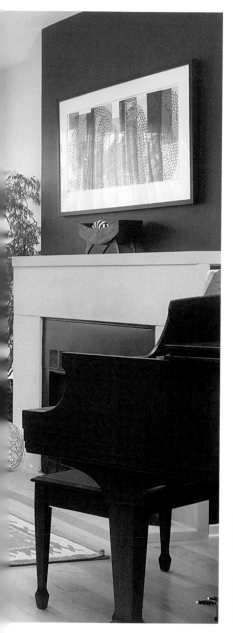

Past Future
Chicago, Old Town

Having grown up with Danish design, the owner of this townhome in Chicago's acclaimed Old Town took a change of lifestyle as a cue to take a new look at Danish Modern. In bringing back the good and the familiar and blending it with existing contemporary Italian and other new French pieces, an interesting fresh look was created for the house. A curator of the decorative arts, the owner was attracted by the clean lines and the Danish ability to marry modern production methods with hand finishes. She let her eye and instinct do the rest, wonderfully integrating family artwork created by her father.

A glimpse of a Jacob Kjaer easy chair from the 1930s and Johannes Andersen's rosewood bar from the mid-twentieth-century with contemporary French furnishings in the den overlooking the outdoor garden. The contemporary pillow is by Finnish designer Anne Kyyro Quinn.

Ole Wanscher's Rungstedlund armchairs from 1967 surround a contemporary Italian table by Ballabio Elli. Borge Mogensen's Chinese-inspired chest by F. D. B. Mobler/C. M. Madsen in Brazilian rosewood circa 1940s sits in the background.

Facing: In the seating area off the kitchen, an Arne Vodder loveseat in original leather, circa 1960, provides a place of rest and relaxation.

A Hollywood Story
Los Angeles, West Hollywood
Interior Design by Elizabeth Dinkel Design Associates

A movie business investment executive and doctor with a young family live the glamorous life in a West Hollywood period house. What is more natural than mid-century furniture in a Modernist home in the Hollywood hills, one might ask? Perhaps it seems obvious that Danish Modern was fit for the job, but the couple, with matrimonial differences of style (one leaning slightly more modern and one slightly more traditional), nevertheless found the perfect solution in Danish Modern pieces by Ole Wanscher and Nanna Ditzel. While responding to traditional elements of style, these Danish Modern pieces also found natural synthesis in this home with that highly sought-after Hollywood look.

Facing: An Ole Wanscher piecrust table in Brazilian rosewood for A. J. Iversen provides a spectacular image on entering the house, with the outdoor pool seen in the distance. This table grandly extends to sixteen feet—enough for the couple's holiday festivities.

An Asian-inspired mid-century Danish sideboard in Brazilian rosewood, with tambour doors and brass-capped feet, blends wonderfully in this Sinatra-era home. Anyone for a martini?

Ole Wanscher's PJ412 chair in Brazilian rosewood, designed circa 1950–1960, occupies a living room overlooking the Hollywood Hills.

Ole Wanscher Asian-inspired ladder-back chairs by A. J. Iversen, 1942, surround a contemporary table off the living room.

Ole Wanscher Asian-inspired ladder-back chairs by A. J. Iversen, 1942, in front of the hallway leading to the private areas of the house.

In the background in this open living/dining space lies a Borge Mogensen modular chest in teak designed in the 1940s and produced by F. D. B. Mobler/C. M. Madsen.

Desert Cool
Palm Springs
Interior Design by Gregga, Jordan, Smiezny

An infusion of great Danish design in a classic Palm Springs period retreat imbues this home-away-from-home with comfort and style. While the home fits neatly into the genre for which Palm Springs is known, given its heyday in the 1950s, the designer fused a mix of early and later modernism in this house with contemporary finishes to give the interior a contextual yet still "now" feel. The house, though modest in scale, has achieved a larger look by the profuse use of art, color, and furniture to achieve drama and comfort at the same time.

In the area from the entrance to the living room, a large Frits Henningsen storage piece in mahogany on neoclassical-influenced legs is tucked in an alcove on the right.

Live and Love
San Francisco
Interior Design by Ken Fulk Design

An eclectic collector with an eye for the dramatic and a passion for life calls this wonderful loft overlooking the Golden Gate City home. In a city of abundant style, the lady of the house and her designer achieved a truly divine mix of the inspired led by their own guts and intuition. Danish Modern was not the objective but rather the result of their affinity to style and was fused with whatever else existed or had found their eyes. From the iconic Egg Chair by Arne Jacobsen to the earlier style of little known Alfred Sjkot-Pedersen, the pieces called to them and intermingled well with the other furnishings. Natural tones, the beautiful patina of the walnut sofa and leather chair, and the clean, organic forms marry brilliantly in this home overlooking the Bay.

An Ole Wanscher PJ412 chair in Brazilian rosewood designed in 1950–1960 sits behind a Swedish desk of macassar ebony from the 1930s.

Facing: This unique sofa in burled walnut by Danish architect Alfred Sjkot-Pedersen was custom designed for his home in the 1930s.

Southern Light
Dallas, Highland Park
Interior Design by Emily Summers

A Dallas area philanthropist and socialite's home, originally built in the 1970s and recently brought up to date, sets the stage for a collection of contemporary art, ceramics, and modernist furniture. With large entertaining spaces and the natural surroundings, the home feels light and airy but also part of its forested area. Ole Wanscher and Hans Wegner provide the infusion of Scandinavian furniture, a large Swedish early-twentieth-century rug spans the living room overlooking Turtle Creek, and a mix of ceramics by Axel Salto and others complements the overall décor and stunning architecture.

Facing: In the entrance, an American table of contemporary provenance and a selection of twentieth-century Danish ceramics blend with the dramatic view of the forest and creek.

In a seating area off the living room, Ole Wanscher tufted chairs produced by A. J. Iversen flank a Brazilian rosewood table by Wanscher for Ilums Bolighus. The chairs, often used by the owner when practicing music, combine style with comfort.

Vibration, a circa 1982 ceramic hanging by American Anne Barnes, provides the backdrop for Axel Salto's fruit form piece with sung glaze for Royal Copenhagen on the dining table.

Facing: A Swedish carpet circa 1929 provides a moment of pattern in the dramatic living room. A Danish ceramic piece rests in the foreground.

The Nordic Door: Villibonk
Door County, Wisconsin
Architecture by David Salmela, Minnesota-based architect of Finnish descent

A second home for urbanite Chicagoans (one of whom is of pure Swedish descent), this space in Northern Wisconsin's Scandinavian-rooted Door County is meant as a respite for the family to reconnect to nature and to a less complicated life. The owners had seen the Finnish architect's work years before and dreamed of living in a house built by him. With one well-placed and insistent phone call to an already busy architect, they were able to persuade him to make their dreams come true. Somewhat later, with the project still in the early stages, the couple stumbled on Borge Mogensen's Spanish Chairs long before they were ready for them—but they instinctively knew the chairs were destined for the house. From there, as they say, the rest is history and the interior had set off in a clear direction.

With architecture strongly influenced by the Finnish-Scandinavian vernacular and great furniture by Danish master furniture designer Borge Mogensen in this retreat, life cannot get any better or simpler.

Vintage Borge Mogensen Spanish Chairs #2226 in natural bull hide leather, designed in 1959 and produced by Fredericia, sit in style with a contemporary sofa and pillows by young Danish designers Urbanite Copenhagen and Yo-Yo Kjaer.

Market Guide:
The *Art* of Collecting

Collecting in the grand old-school way of building focused collections is, to a large degree, a diminished one in much of the decorative arts today. Today's modus operandi has much more to do with the eclecticism that is so in vogue in interior design. Furniture collections are increasingly based on one-off moments of interest and general fashion than on a studied and curatorial approach to buying. While showing a mark of self-confidence in terms of going with what catches the eye, this approach also leaves the consumer more and more in the hands of the "experts."

Danish Easy Chair and
ottoman of elm and
mohair, circa 1960s.

The "Production" Version:
Ole Wanscher Vertical 3 X-back sidechair for Ilums Bolighus. Shown in rosewood. The chair is of nice quality but does not command the price of the cabinet-maker's version. Both have been reupholstered impacting the chair only marginally as the uphol-stery is incidental to the piece.

The advent of the Internet has created price transparency in the field the likes of which has never existed before, but it also has made an understanding of the contemporaneous price based upon an Internet image of a piece unseen by the buyer, a false substitute for a real and solid understanding of the collecting field.

What You Should Know

As the market for twentieth-century Scandinavian design matures, there has been an increase in the awareness of the different designers and cabinetmakers, driven largely by a few big designer names. This is a reflection of the times we live in, where designers have become celebrities and is counter to the period itself

The "Cabinetmaker's" Version:
Ole Wanscher X-back dining chair shown in Brazilian rosewood, 1942. Manufactured by A. J. Iversen. This chair commands a premium due to the refined execution of the handcraftsmanship.

when Arne Jacobsen proclaimed, "People buy a chair to sit in and they don't really care who designed it." Nevertheless, the first wave or resurgence in Nordic design started with Arne Jacobsen, Hans Wegner, and Finn Juhl—those designers who had the most exposure to the U.S. market through distribution or manufacture during the period itself. More recently, there has been a phenomenal interest in Poul Kjaerholm, a designer who only produced about twenty different models during the period he was designing, but whose designs have been in continuous production through the years and have had some distribution in the U.S. as well. The field is obviously deeper than just those four designers and I have tried to give a broader overview in this book.

Designer and Cabinetmaker

Generally, what determines the value of any piece is the interplay of designer, rarity, condition, and cabinetmaker. Add provenance and you definitely have a winner! I personally have never been impressed by provenance, other than to determine authenticity, so that is not something I find particularly desirable. But that is probably a reflection of my Midwestern values and is not reflective of how the broader market tends to view the matter. The name-brand designers should be familiar to you by this point: Kaare Klint, Ole Wanscher, Borge Mogensen, Poul Kjaerholm, Finn Juhl, Arne Jacobsen, Hans Wegner, Frits Henningsen, Jacob Kjaer, and Mogens Koch. Peder Moos, on whom we have not focused here, is another important designer to look for but who only produced a limited amount of work. There are many others, but their body of work is mostly more modest.

Any of the top twenty-six or so cabinetmakers represented by the Cabinetmakers' Guild are generally very high quality and worth considering for your home or collection. However, unless it is an unusual or unique piece, it is currently the combination of designer and cabinetmaker that actually will make a difference in terms of price. This leaves some good buying opportunities if the cabinetmaker is excellent and the piece is desirable but the designer is unknown or lesser known.

Ole Wanscher is a good example for comparison of the difference a cabinetmaker makes to desirability. He was one of the first designers to grasp the power of self-imitation to enhance the earning potential of a design. By streamlining the styling of his own pieces for larger scale production, he was thus able to broaden his appeal. The X-back chair (shown on pages 198 and 199) was produced by top cabinetmaker A. J. Iversen as well as issued in a department store version for Ilums Bolighus, Copenhagen's main design center.

While both chairs are made of Brazilian rosewood, the quality and craftsmanship of the Iversen piece is of a much higher level and rarer while the Ilums Bolighus version is simply very good quality. Both are wonderful examples of his designs and would make a great addition to almost any home, but the buyer seeking the Iversen version will pay a significant premium.

Vintage or New?

With many of the iconic designs being reissued under licenses and knockoffs
of those same designs being made and imported from Asia. what is the consumer to do? For both moral and aesthetic reasons. I personally would not buy
a knockoff under any circumstances. You get what you pay for in life. and the
quality of a knockoff is likely to be poor and will do nothing for our environment once you throw it away. But after that, my motto has always simply been:
buy the best that you can afford. If a rare vintage chair with original leather in
excellent condition is out of the question for you financially. then buying a
licensed reissue or a chair still being produced is perfectly acceptable. Also.

Kaare Klint RR#5011
(three-seater), shown
in Cuban mahogany
and original vintage
leather, 1935.
Manufactured by Rudolf
Rasmussen, this piece is
highly sought after and
commands a premium
price.

some of us just like new things versus old things and that is okay—you should buy what you like. But a few words on the pecking order of value from highest to lowest:

- Mint condition with original leather or horsehair—Vintage furniture by the great designers/cabinetmakers in mint original condition and original leather/horsehair is going to have the highest value in today's market. The premium placed on the leather alone is going to be very significant and will wither away when the leather eventually wears out. You need to recognize this when contemplating your purchase.

- Mint or good original condition (with new upholstery if seating)

- Minimal conservation and/or restoration (with new upholstery if seating)

- Refinished (with new upholstery if seating)

Depending on the item, the market price of new furniture may be more or less than the vintage. Note that reissues can impair the value of vintage pieces if the same quality standards are being upheld and it is still in production by the original maker; however, this really depends on the piece and the quantities available. There are a lot of variables here associated with condition, wood type, and upholstery in looking at new versus vintage pieces that are discussed later in this section. But what is generally true is that the resale for new furniture is almost always less than for vintage. New furniture being resold tends to get lumped in with "used" furniture even if it is by a famous designer, and the market values that accordingly.

New production version of Hans Wegner's Seminal Ox Chair EJ 100 by Erik Jorgensen, designed 1960, has less value than an original by Johannes Hansen in leather.

Woods

> "Here in the North we are more or less approaching the same
> style—with the reservation that the well to do will have more
> room and can choose a better quality, or shall we say a better
> sort of wood? But the upper classes don't really have to choose
> a more boastful furniture style than ordinary people anymore."
>
> — *Poul Henningsen*[1]

There is a common misconception that all Scandinavian furniture is light wooded.
It is true that the Swedes (think Bruno Mathsson) and the Finns (think Alvar
Aalto) used a fair bit of blond wood because that was native to their lands. The
Danes used a fair bit of it too, although the middle classes had an aversion to
lighter woods until Borge Mogensen and others popularized oak and beech and
Finn Juhl introduced teak. And, to give myth some credit when it comes to teak,
the Danes were the biggest importers of it after World War II. It is a lovely wood
with a bad reputation caused by all of the copies and knockoffs during the period.
Remember, wood is a natural resource—in general, there are no bad woods, just
bad cabinetmakers (or factories). That is not to say that there aren't prized
woods—Brazilian rosewood is a highly beautiful and desirable wood, but what
really makes the difference is the quality of craftsmanship, the selection of the
actual pieces of wood used, and the rarity of the piece. The most prized woods
used were the hardwoods Brazilian rosewood and Cuban mahogany, both of
which are virtually extinct for the purposes of modern production. But, all else
being equal, a piece by a top cabinetmaker in rosewood is going to be more valuable than a production piece in rosewood (as in the earlier example). The same is
true of teak. A top-quality piece in teak can nevertheless be worth much more
than a nice production piece made of rosewood.

Easy chair in Brazilian
rosewood and original
caning designed as part
of a living room set for
Bernt/Worts in the mid-
twentieth-century. While a
production piece, it is
high quality and is available at attractive prices
in today's market.

Veneers vs. Solid Woods

There is a great deal of confusion over the desirability of veneered versus solid wood furniture. For many people, the word *veneer* conjures up associations of cheap laminate furniture that bubbles and peels. In reality, the art of veneering has been around for centuries and is not indicative in and of itself of quality.

Cabinetmakers may choose to use a wood veneer for a variety of reasons. The first is decorative. By using a veneer, a cabinetmaker is able to choose a particular grain pattern and repeat that pattern (a method known as book matching) across a tabletop or front of a cabinet. This process produces a much more visually consistent surface than trying to match individual pieces of wood. Veneer is also used for inlay. Inlay is a process in which pieces of a contrasting wood or grain are pieced together to create a decorative pattern. This can be as simple as adding detailing around the edges of a tabletop. More complex inlay that involves placing pieces of veneer to create pictures or intricate patterns is referred to as marquetry.

Top-quality Ole Wanscher piecrust dining table by A. J. Iversen in Brazilian rosewood. The top is veneer with inlays and the legs are solid. Tops are often in veneer with support structures like legs in hardwood. But what makes this piece special is not only the design but also the selection of the veneer and the craftsmanship.

Veneer can also be used to solve problems of stability. Some woods, such as ebony, can be brittle and not suitable for use in certain capacities. However, that wood may still be used as a veneer over a more stable surface. In addition, veneer is not as susceptible to changes in humidity and temperature as solid wood. This decreases the chance that the wood will split and separate or warp during the dry winter months or swell during spring and summer.

It is true that veneer can also be used as a cost-saving measure. When a cabinet-maker is creating a piece of furniture, especially if he or she is working with a rare or expensive wood, he may use a veneer on the exposed surfaces in order to save on the cost of raw materials. In terms of actual quality of the piece, this is mainly relevant with cheap industrially produced furniture where veneers have become so thin that they have a very short useful life.

There are, of course, drawbacks to the use of veneer. If it is not applied properly, there is the chance that the veneer can separate from the underlying material. In addition, once the surface veneer has been damaged, it can be difficult to repair or refinish if it is too thin.

Almost all of the Danish furniture designs discussed here are of a higher quality and the veneer can be conserved or restored.

Types of Wood Used in Danish Modern Furniture

Identification of wood can be tricky even for the most seasoned of us. There is great diversity in the types of woods and the regions in which they are found. Color varies by region and patination changes it further. Trees, being natural living things, can have unique features. One thing that is helpful is that the Scandinavians used a few main types of wood. Therefore, with a little training as to the woods, it is generally easy to determine. Of course, knowledge of the designer, cabinetmaker, and the period in which the piece was produced is also of great benefit. In the cabinetmaker and high-quality production pieces from the period, we mainly see the following types of wood:

Brazilian Rosewood *(Dalbergia nigra)*.

Other names: jacaranda, jacaranda preto (Brazil), palissander, palissandre du Brazil (France). As its name implies, this species is native to Brazil. It is characterized by a color that can vary from chocolate to violet streaked with black. The grain is generally straight although it can be wavy. Rosewood is considered a hardwood and is very durable. Due to the strength of the wood and its oily nature, rosewood can be challenging to work with. It is difficult to achieve a highly polished surface without a great deal of care. Brazilian rosewood is now considered an endangered species and is protected by CITES (the Convention on International Trade in Endangered Species of Wild Fauna and Flora). Most of what is on today's market is Indian rosewood, technically a different species but with a similar look.

While there are other species of rosewood, Brazilian rosewood was used almost exclusively during the mid-century period. The A. J. Iversen pieces are usually exquisite because of the fine craftsmanship employed, but pieces by Jacob Kjaer and the other top cabinetmakers can be equally as remarkable. Many of the Danish production pieces can also be beautiful if a particularly beautiful grain

Round coffee table of Brazilian rosewood, circa 1960. Manufactured by Heltborg.

was selected and there was an element of hand-finish to them. In general, pieces in Brazilian rosewood are rarest because this wood was the most expensive. But the design often leads to the choice of wood, and some pieces simply look better or are equally as nice in other woods. Note that later production pieces in the late 1960s and 1970s used proxies to simulate rosewood, as it became increasingly expensive and difficult to source. It is usually obvious—these pieces have a brownish tinge as reddish dyes do not age well.

Mahogany.

There are many different species of the hardwood mahogany. Cuban mahogany is most prized, African a nice proxy. Sapele, often used after World War II, is considered a light mahogany. The types, representing the most common found in Danish Modern furniture, are summarized below.

Jacaranda and black lacquered cabinet, 1930. Gustave Axel Berg Cabinet, Sweden.

• **Cuban mahogany** *(Swietenia mahagoni).* Also known as Spanish mahogany, Cuban mahogany was favored by cabinetmakers from the seventeenth century until the early twentieth century for its beautiful reddish brown color, exquisite figuring, natural luster, and strength. As a historical footnote, there are those who claim that the "Cuban" mahogany used in eighteenth-century French furniture was actually from Santo Domingo given the French connections to that island, but this doesn't ultimately detract from the merits and beauty of actual Cuban mahogany. The popularity of this wood caused it to be harvested to the brink of extinction. In 1946, Cuba banned the export of this wood in order to allow the remaining trees to regenerate. Although a small amount of this wood is now available in the current market, it is protected by CITES and is still considered endangered.

Most of Kaare Klint's pieces made before World War II are of Cuban mahogany and are highly sought after because of the richness of the wood. Rudolf Rasmussen is the main cabinetmaker with whom Klint collaborated. Klint believed in leaving the surface uncolored so that it would gradually age and develop a natural patina, employing only wax polish to protect the wood and give it sheen. Many of Klint's designs have been in continuous production,

European Walnut.

Other names: Named after the country of origin: English, French, Italian, etc. European walnut is generally found in earlier pieces from the 1930s and reissue pieces in the late century (using American walnut). The color varies according to origin and is usually gray-brown with a darker color of smoky brown, almost black. The grain is straight to wavy (unlike American walnut) with a rather course texture. With patination, it becomes a lighter golden color with smoky black streaks.

Frits Henningsen executive desk in walnut, circa 1930. Manufactured by Frits Henningsen.

Teak *(Tectona grandis).*

Other names: mai sak, pahi, sagwan, tekku, kyun jati sak, djati, gia thi. Teak is a hardwood native to South and Southeast Asia. It is not a rainforest wood, as is commonly thought, but rather thrives in the seasonally dry tropics. Its grain is characteristically golden brown with darker chocolate brown striations. As teak ages, the striations fade and the overall color mellows. It is a very durable wood and is very oily, making it suitable for indoor and outdoor furniture, boat building, and decks. Due to the enormous demand for it in the late 1940s and 1950s, it became overused and deforested. It is now harvested on environmentally sustainable plantations. Teak was used extensively in Danish Modern furniture throughout the period. Bangkok teak was often employed in tabletops and cabinet pieces for the beauty of its natural grain and its resistance to scratches and stains.

For comparison purposes, this cabinet is shown in both Brazilian rosewood and teak. The rosewood is red and black whereas teak tends to be slightly more orange with streaks of black. Svend Langkilde designed storage cabinets for Langkilde Mobler in rosewood and teak, circa 1960. Fading through exposure to sunlight can tend to diminish the differences, making it harder to tell superficially. If you are unsure, look at the figuring of the wood and the extremities of a piece less exposed to sunlight.

European Beech *(Fagus sylvatica)*.

Other names: English, French, Danish, etc., according to country of origin. Native to the region, beech is used by many designers from the period such as Bruno Mathsson. Beech naturally has a pale pink-brown color; however, it is a common practice in Europe to steam the wood until it develops a darker reddish-brown tone. In addition to changing the color, the steaming makes the wood easier to work with. Beech has a straight grain and a very even tone. Over time and exposure to sun, the color can darken slightly. Beech is a very durable hardwood that is resistant to compression and splitting, making it ideal for bending. It takes a variety of finishes well.

Carl Malmsten sofa with beechwood legs.

matter is that if you bought something recently, you are unlikely to have a gain large enough to offset the transaction costs of selling it again. The dealer or auction house that buys it back or takes it on consignment is going to need to be compensated for doing so and you will likely lose some of your money. You may still end up better off than if you were to buy new furniture and sell it to someone else, but the overall goal is not to lose money.

Purchasing over the Internet

Sourcing has never been easier. It would seem that collector's piece you want is only a Google away, be it by auction or from a traditional dealer. As one interior designer recently lamented, there are no secret resources anymore (well, perhaps that is a slight exaggeration). Indeed, the Internet has brought an unprecedented amount of information and transparency to the market, a trend certain to continue as search engines and Web technology becomes better. One can venture from Copenhagen to New York to Sydney on a shopping spree within seconds, a feat unimaginable only a few years ago. While there are regional pricing differences (as a result of supply and demand) that need to be factored in against transportation costs and the risk of an unpleasant surprise if the piece does not turn out to be as spectacular as the image, the basic value drivers are the same as always: designer, rarity, condition, cabinetmaker, and provenance. Buyers and sellers need to ensure they do business with trusted sources. The following are several tips for buying over the Internet.

Pictures can be deceiving. Photos are critical—even when there is no attempt to present something different from how it actually is, the camera often has its own view of a piece. Average pieces can look spectacular because of the situation in which they are photographed, and some of the most beautiful pieces may, for whatever reason, fall flat in an image. Patina and feel rarely translate, certainly when it comes to testing the comfort of a piece or seeing the beauty of wood. Relying on Web sites alone is almost never the best idea, but if a visit to see the pieces is out of the question, obtaining high-resolution images or multiple views is a good idea. Serious clients should not be shy about requesting them along with as

Facing: Vintage Rungstedlund sideboard and coffee table by Ole Wanscher from the mid-twentieth-century. While both are in Brazilian rosewood, the sideboard has been completely restored and is much deeper in color while the coffee table has patination associated with exposure to use and sunlight.

Dust weekly—that's all! Danish Modern furniture requires similar care as furniture from earlier periods. But it is important to understand that one is caring for the thin surface coating and not the wood itself. Dusting weekly with a dry or very lightly moistened cloth is generally sufficient. Using any modern cleaners other than what is recommended by the dealer or your restorer is likely to be detrimental to the piece; chemicals from these commercial cleaners, especially those that contain silicone, seep into the surface of the wood and become embedded. For simple care, a good quality paste wax is recommended to add a sheen and protection that is easily removed. Every six months or so you may wish to do the following to conserve your furniture:

- Rosewood, mahogany, and walnut—Polish with any natural wax if desired.

- Teak—The natural beauty of oil-finish teak used in Danish Modern furniture can be maintained by applying modest quantities of boiled linseed oil from time to time.

- Oak—To keep oak clean, wipe with a cloth dipped in mild soap and water and wrung dry. Polish with any natural wax if desired.

Leather—moisturize seasonally. Good leather ages well and develops a patina. It may not last quite as long but, like wood, it does not need much care—it is like your skin and can use moisturizing periodically. Edelman Leathers suggests the use of saddle soap, castile oil mixed with water, or Lexol conditioner seasonally. It is best normally to test the product first in an unexposed area. Leather can crack; on vintage pieces, that may detract from value if it becomes too serious, but don't overmoisturize and, by all means, don't use anything abrasive. A soft sponge or cloth should be fine.

Horsehair—let it live. Horsehair, made from the hair on the tail of horses, is often used on Danish furniture. It has a nice sheen and is highly durable, with a useful life of one hundred years. It is best left to age naturally.

Protect from sunlight. Always remember that sunlight, which has a high ultraviolet content, will cause woods to fade and finishes to break down. Southern exposure of sunlight is usually the strongest. The amount of time necessary for serious fading is variable, depending on the wood used, the type of colorant used to stain the wood, and other environmental factors. Red is the most fugitive of all the colors, so red mahogany will show signs of fading faster than walnut. Also the colorant used in the finishes fades, with red again being the quickest. A constant strong direct exposure can cause damage in a matter of months. The simplest remedy is best—close draperies and curtains when away. There are also UV protectant films that can be added to window glass, eliminating up to 98 percent of ultraviolet rays. They have greatly improved over the years and are not detectable.

Ole Wanscher X-back chair with Chinese and English influence in Brazilian rosewood produced by cabinetmaker A. J. Iversen with original leather.

Humidity: 40–60 percent is ideal. Unlike English and Chinese antiques, Danish furniture seems to respond reasonably well to changes in humidity like those found in the northern part of the United States. Leather can crack and should be treated seasonally as indicated previously. A humidifier is recommended in winter in northern climates—both for your skin and the furniture—but major problems are rare with Danish Modern.

By and large, Danish Modern furniture was built to last. Indeed, pieces by the top cabinetmakers are probably some of the greatest of all time and certainly of the twentieth century; there are very few cabinetmakers of this kind left in the world today. Treated with a modicum of respect, Danish Modern pieces can continue to be passed down from generation to generation. While this may seem anathema in today's market, I believe quality will always have a place. One American furniture maker recently asked an editor of a national shelter magazine how he could get his clients to understand that the high price was a reflection of the built-to-last quality of the furniture his firm produces. The response: "What makes you think the American consumer wants furniture to last forever?" While humorous and indicative of the times in which we live, I can't believe that the world won't eventually catch on to a more reasoned way of life on this resource-scarce planet in which we live. Maybe with greater attention to our environment and eventual fatigue from constant change in our lives, some traditional values will return.

But current trends aside, my own prejudice is that you need to love any piece and want to live with it for a long time before buying it. In terms of value, remember these five simple drivers when purchasing a piece of Danish Modern: designer, rarity, condition, cabinetmaker, and provenance. From there, if conservation is needed, take it to a trusted source and let him or her do the job. Then just enjoy your piece, dusting occasionally with intermittent polishing.

Facing: Vintage Danish cabinetmaker sofa from the 1930s in European walnut. The piece was found in original condition and needed only to be polished and reupholstered.

Endnotes

Danish Modern Furniture: Roots and Development

1 McFadden, *Scandinavian Modern*, 14.
2 Glambek, "One of the age's noblest cultural movements," 71.
3 Ibid., 71–72.
4 "Training in Furniture Design."
5 Klint, *Mobilia*, no. 55.
6 Henningsen, *Mobilia*, no. 56–57.
7 Hiort, "Design and Function."
8 Kampmann, *Arts of Denmark*, 7.
9 Knox, "Long Awaited Museum Show Opens," 1, 14.
10 Henningsen, *Mobilia*, no. 54.

Global Infusions: Why Danish Modern Mixes So Well

1 Wanscher, *Art of Furniture*, 9.
2 Wanscher, *Art of Furniture*, 11.
3 Ibid.
4 Ibid., 12.
5 Ibid.
6 Noritsugu, *Danish Chairs*, 72.
7 Wanscher, *Art of Furniture*, 15.
8 Ibid.
9 Ibid., 17.
10 Handler, *Ming Furniture*, 111.
11 Ibid.
12 Rasmussen, *Modern Danish Design*, 138.
13 Davies, *Twentieth Century Danish Furniture Design and the English Vernacular*, 44.
14 Hepplewhite, *Cabinetmaker & Upholsterer's Guide*, preface.
15 Davies, *Norwegian Wood*, 87.
16 Davies, *Twentieth Century Danish Furniture Design and the English Vernacular*, 46.
17 Ibid., 48.
18 Andrews and Andrews, *Religion in Wood*, 7.
19 Ibid., 8.
20 Sprigg, *Shaker Hands*, 33.

Cabinetmakers' Guild: Selected Designer and Cabinetmaker Briefs (1927–1966)

1 Karlsen, *Furniture Designed by Borge Mogensen*, 12.
2 Jalk, *Danish Furniture 1927–1936*, 142.
3 Ibid., 196.
4 Jalk, *Danish Furniture 1957–1966*, 198.
5 Ibid., 238.
6 Jalk, *Danish Furniture 1957–66*, 56.
7 Jalk, *Danish Furniture 1947–56*, 196.
8 Karlsen, *Furniture Designed by Borge Mogensen*, 11.
9 Ibid., 74.
10 Bernsen, *Dansk Design Center*, 106.
11 Ibid., 102.
12 Jacobsen, *Dansk Design Center*, 67.
13 Ibid., 47.
14 Hiort, *Finn Juhl: A Biography by Esbjorn Hiort*, 8.
15 Rudolf Rasmussen historical booklet about the company.
16 Sheridan, *Poul Kjaerholm: Furniture Architect*, preface.
17 *Danish Furniture 1947–1956*, 144.
18 *Danish Furniture 1957–1966*, 306.
19 Jalk, *Danish Furniture 1927–1936*, 76.
20 Ibid., 138.
21 *Danish Furniture 1927–1936*, 204.
22 Ibid., 216.
23 Ibid.

A Market Guide: The Art of Collecting

1 Henningsen, *Mobilia*, no. 56–57, March-April 1960

Resource Guide

Twentieth-Century Danish Modern Dealers

Andrew Hollingsworth
222 West Huron
Chicago, IL 60610
(312) 440–9554 (phone)
www.andrewhollingsworth.com

Antik
104 Franklin Street
New York, NY 10013
(212) 343–0471 (phone)
www.antik-nyc.net

Arenskjold
623 Warren Street
Hudson, NY 12534
(518) 828–2800 (phone)
www.arenskjold.com

Dansk Mobelkunst
Bredgade 32
DK–1260 Copenhagen, Denmark
+45 33 32 38 37 (phone)
www.dmk.dk

Denmark 50
7974 Melrose Ave.
Los Angeles, CA 90046
(323) 852–1939 (phone)
www.denmark50.com

Good Design
784 Park Avenue
New York, NY 10001
(212) 570–9914 (phone)
www.gooddesignshop.com

Hedge
48 Gold Street
San Francisco, CA 94133
(415) 433–2233 (phone)
www.hedgegallery.com

House of Design
Bredgade 21
DK–1260 Copenhagen, Denmark
+45 3333 0300 (phone)
www.houseofdesign.dk

Jackson Design Ab
Sibyllegatan 53
SE-114 43 Stockholm, Sweden
+46 8 665 33 50 (phone)
www.jacksons.se

J. F. Chen
8414 Melrose Ave
Los Angeles, CA 90069
(323) 655–6310 (phone)
www.jfchen.com

Jorgen L. Dalgaard
Bredgade 28 (Odd Fellow Palaeet)
DK-1260 Copenhagen, Denmark
+45 33 14 09 05 (phone)
www.jdalgaard.dk

Klassik
Bredgade 3
DK-1260 Copenhagen, Denmark
+45 33 33 90 60 (phone)
www.klassik.dk

Kolmorgen ApS.
Valhojs Alle 152
DL-2610 Rodovre, Denmark
+45 20 63 43 67 (phone)
www.kolmorgen.com

Modernity
Sibyllegatan 6
114 42 Stockholm, Sweden
+46 8 20 80 25 (phone)
www.modernity.se

Paere Dansk
13 Stratford Road
Kensington
London W8 6RF
England
+44 77 71 86 19 39 (phone)
www.paeredansk.com

Philippe Denys
ARTUS S.A.
45 Ave. Wielemans Ceuppens
1190 Bruxelles
+32 25 12 36 07 (phone)
www.philippedenys.com

Wyeth (to the trade only)
315 Spring Street
New York, NY 10013
(212) 243–3661 (phone)

1st Dibs
www.1stdibs.com
Lists many American and European
dealers of Danish Modern

Current Manufacturers/Distributors

Note: dealer locations can be found
on manufacturer's Web sites.

Brayton International
250 Swathmore Ave.
High Point, NC 27263
(336) 434–4151 (phone)
www.brayton.com
Designers represented: Finn Juhl,
Hans J. Wegner

Carl Hansen
5560 Holnevaenget 8
5560 Aarup, Denmark
+45 6612 1404 (phone)
www.carlhansen.com
Designers represented: Hans J. Wegner

Fredericia
Treldevej 183
7000 Fredericia, Denmark
+45 75 92 33 44 (phone)
www.fredericia.com
Designers represented: Borge Mogensen,
Hans J. Wegner, Nanna Ditzel

Fritz Hansen
Allerødvej 8
DK–3450 Allerød, Denmark
+45 48 17 23 00 (phone)
www.fritzhansen.com
Designers represented: Hans J. Wegner,
Arne Jacobsen

P. J. Furniture A/S
Højerupvej 30
DK–4660 Store-Heddinge, Denmark
+45 5650 2175 (phone)
www.pj-furniture.com
Designers represented: Ole Wanscher

Rudolf Rasmussen
Noerrebrogade 45
DK–2200 Copenhagen N, Denmark
+45 3539 6233 (phone)
www.rudrasmussen.dk
Designers represented: Kaare Klint, Mogens
Koch, Borge Mogensen, Hans J. Wegner

Auction Houses

Blomqvist Kunsthandel
Tordenskioldsgate 5
N–0160 Oslo, Norway
+47 2270 8770 (phone)
www.blomqvist.no

Bruun Rasmussen
Bredgade 33
1260 Copenhagen K, Denmark
+45 3343 6911 (phone)
www.bruun-rasmussen.dk

Bukowski's Finland
Bukowski Oy Ab
Stora Robertsgatan 12
SF–00120 Helsingfors
+35 8 9 668 91 10 (phone)
www.bukowskis.fi

Bukowski's Sweden
Arsenalsgatan 4
Box 1754
111 87 Stockholm, Sweden
+46 8 614 08 00 (phone)
www.bukowskis.se

Crafoord Auktioner
Clemenstorget 7
SE–222 21 Lund, Sweden
+46 46 211 18 70 (phone)
www.crafoords.com

Gauguin Auktioner Aps
Vesterlundvej 15
2730 Herlev, Denmark
+45 45 35 11 12 (phone)
www.gauguin.dk

Lauritz.com
Dynamovej 11
2730 Herlev, Denmark
+45 44 50 98 50 (phone)
www.lauritz.com

Los Angeles Modern Auctions
PO Box 56748
Sherman Oaks, CA 91413
(323) 904–1950 (phone)
www.lamodern.com

Phillips De Pury & Company
450 West 15 St.
New York, NY 10011
(212) 940–1200 (phone)
www.phillipsdepury.com

Quittenbaum Munich
Theresinstrasse 60
D-80333 Muenchen, Germany
+49 89 273702125 (phone)
www.quittenbaum.de

Rago Arts and Auction Center
333 N. Main St.
Lambertville, NJ 08530
(609) 397–9374 (phone)
www.ragoarts.com

Shapiro Auctioneers
162 Queen Street
Woollahra NSW 2025
Australia
(612) 9326 1588 (phone)
www.shapiroauctioneers.com.au

Sotheby's
1334 York Ave. at 72nd St.
New York, NY 10021
(212) 606–7000 (phone)
www.sothebys.com

Wright
1440 West Hubbard
Chicago, IL 60622
(312) 563–0020 (phone)
www.wright20.com

Decorators Using the Style

Elizabeth Dinkel Design Associates, Inc.
554 Norwich Dr.
West Hollywood, CA 90048
(310) 278–3700 (phone)

Emily Summers Design Associates
4639 Insurance Ln.
Dallas, TX 75205
(214) 871–9669 (phone)
www.emilysummers.com

Gregga, Jordan, Smiezny, Inc.
1255 N. State Pkwy.
Chicago, IL 60610
(312) 787–0017 (phone)
www.gjsinc.com
Design team: Alex Jordan and Dan Smiezny

Insight Environmental Designs
1997 Lake Ave.
Highland Park, IL 60035
(847) 432–4606 (phone)
Design team: Anne Kaplan
and Bruce Goers

Ken Fulk Design
4104 Twenty-fourth Street #221
San Francisco, CA 94114
(415) 285–1164 (phone)
www.kenfulkdesign.com

SemelSnow Interior Design
223 West Erie #7 NW
Chicago, IL 60610
(312) 640–0000 (phone)
www.semelsnow.com
Design team: Arlene Semel and
Brian Snow

Shawn Henderson Interior Design
118 E. Twenty-eighth St., Ste. 701
New York, NY 10016
(212) 253–8473 (phone)
www.shawnhenderson.com

Architects
Using the Style

David Salmela Architect
630 West Fourth Street
Duluth, MN 55806
(218) 724–7517 (phone)
www.salmelaarchitect.com

Museums

Cooper-Hewitt National Design Museum
Smithsonian Institution
2 East 91st Street
New York, NY 10128
(212) 860–6868 (phone)
www.si.edu/ndm

Danish Design Centre
HC Andersens Boulevard 27
DK-1553 Copenhagen V
+45 3369 3369 (phone)
www.ddc.dk

Danish Furniture Index (managed by Danish Museum of Art and Design) www.furnitureindex.dk
Listing of all the important Danish Modern designers and their designs with robust search capability

Danish Museum of Art and Design
Bregaede 68
1260 Copenhagen K, Denmark
+45 33 18 56 56 (phone)
www.kunstindustrimuseet.dk

The Museum of Modern Art
11 W. 53rd St.
New York, NY 10019
(212) 708–9400 (phone)
www.moma.org

Official Website of Denmark
Information on Danish design, exhibitions, galleries, etc.
www.denmark.dk

Trapholt Museum
Æblehaven 23
DK 6000 Kolding, Denmark
+45 76 30 05 30 (phone)
www.trapholt.dk

Vitra Design Museum
Charles-Eames-Strausse 1
D-79576 Weil am Rhein, Germany
www.design-museum.com
+49 7621 702 3640 (phone)

Conservation

Deller Conservation
2600 Keslinger Road
Geneva, IL 60134
(630) 232-1708 (phone)
www.deller.com

Bibliography/ Resource Guide

Scandinavian Design

Ellison, Michael and Leslie Piña. *Scandinavian Modern Furnishings 1930–1970: Designed for Life.* Atglen: Schiffer Publishing Ltd., 2002.

Englund, Magnus and Chrystina Schmidt. *Scandinavian Modern.* London: Ryland Peters & Small, 2003.

Fiell, Charlotte and Peter. *Scandinavian Design.* Cologne: Taschen, 2002.

Halén, Widar and Kerstin Wickman, ed. *Scandinavian Design Beyond the Myth: Fifty Years of Design from the Nordic Countries.* Stockholm: Arvinius Forlag/Form Forlag, 2003.

McFadden, David Revere. "Scandinavian Modern: A Century in Profile," in *Scandinavian Modern Design 1880–1980,* ed. David Revere McFadden, 11–23. New York: Harry N. Abrams, Inc., 1982.

Zahle, Erik, ed. *A Treasury of Scandinavian Design.* New York: Golden Press, 1961.

Danish Design

Hansen, Per and Klaus Petersen. *250 Danske Designmobler: Border, Stole, Sofaer, Lamper, Reoler of Meget Mere.* Aschehoug: Dansk Forlag A/S, 2004.

———. *Dansk Mobelguide: Moderne Danske Mobelklassikere.* Aschehoug: Dansk Forlag A/S, 2003.

Jalk, Grete. *40 Years of Danish Furniture Design: The Copenhagen Cabinet-makers' Guild Exhibitions 1927–1966.* 4 vols. Copenhagen: Teknologisk Instituts Forlag, 1987.

Kampmann, Viggo. *The Arts of Denmark: Viking to Modern.* Denmark: Det Berlingske Bogtrykkeri, 1960.

Oda, Noritsugu. *Danish Chairs.* San Francisco: Chronicle Books, 1999.

Sieck, Frederik. *Danish Furniture Design.* Copenhagen: Nyt Nordisk Forlag Arnold Busck A/S, 1990.

Swedish Design

Boman, Monica, ed. *Design in Sweden.* Translated by Roger G. Tanner. Copenhagen: The Swedish Institute, 1985.

Lindkvist, Lennart, ed. *Design in Sweden.* Translated by Claude Stephenson. Stockholm: The Swedish Institute, 1977.

Individual Designers/Cabinetmakers

Bernsen, Jens. *Hans J. Wegner.* Copenhagen: Danish Design Center, 2001.

Hiort, Esbjorn. *Finn Juhl: Furniture, Architecture, Applied Art.* Translated by Martha Gaber Abrahamsen. Copenhagen: The Danish Architectural Press, 1990.

Karlsen, Arne. *Furniture Designed by Borge Mogensen.* Copenhagen: The Danish Architectural Press, 1968.

Sheridan, Michael. *Poul Kjaerholm: Furniture Architect.* Humlebæk: Louisiana Museum of Modern Art, 2006.

Tojjner, Poul Erik and Kjeld Vindum. *Arne Jacobsen: Architect and Designer.* Copenhagen: Danish Design Center, 1999.

Widman, Dag, Karin Winter, Nina Stritzler-Levine. *Bruno Mathsson: Architect and Designer.* Edited by Lis Hogdal. New Haven: Yale University Press, 2006.

Historical Furniture Styles

Andrews, Edward Deming and Faith Andrews. *Religion in Wood: A Book of Shaker Furniture.* Bloomington: Indiana University Press, 1966.

Andrews, Edward Deming. *Shaker Furniture: The Craftsmanship of an American Communal Sect. 1937.* Reprint. New York: Dover, 1964.

Becksvoort, Christian. *The Shaker Legacy: Perspectives on an Enduring Furniture Style.* Newtown: Taunton Books and Videos, 2000.

Drexler, Arthur and Greta Daniel. *Introduction to Twentieth Century Design from the Collection of the Museum of Modern Art New York.* Garden City: Doubleday & Company, Inc., 1959.

Handler, Sarah. *Ming Furniture: In the Light of Chinese Architecture.* Berkeley: Ten Speed Press, 2005.

Hepplewhite, George. *The Cabinetmaker & Upholsterer's Guide.* New York: Dover Publications, Inc., 1969.

Shixiang, Wang. *Classic Chinese Furniture: Ming and Early Qing Dynasties.* Translated by Sarah Handler and Wang Shixiang. Chicago: Art Media Resources, Ltd., 1991.

Sprigg, June. *By Shaker Hands.* New York: Alfred A Knopf, Inc., 1975.

Riley, Noël and Patricia Bayer, ed. *The Elements of Design: The Development of Design and Stylistic Elements from the Renaissance to the Postmodern Era.* London: Octopus Publishing, 2003.

Wanscher, Ole. *The Art of Furniture: 5000 Years of Furniture and Interiors.* London: George Allen & Unwin Ltd., 1968.

Historical References

Brenner, Douglas. "The Remix: The Other Danish Modern." *New York Times*, April 3, 2005, Design Magazine, Section 6, 36.

Cotter, Holland. "When New Art Was All Called Art Nouveau." *New York Times*, November 5, 2000, Section 2, 21.

"Danish Modern Pieces Put On View in Brooklyn Store." *New York Times*, January 14, 1959, Food Fashions Family Furnishing Section, 23.

"Double Duty Items In Furniture Show; Removable, Reversible Trays in Cocktail

Table Make Handy Unit in Jensen Exhibition." *New York Times*, October 10, 1942, 9.

Fritz Hansen company Web site, "History." http://www.fritzhansen.com/History (accessed February 15, 2007).

"Furniture and Interior Decorations Take Note Of the Centennial Along the Delaware River." *New York Times*, June 19, 1938, *The New York Times Magazine*, 108.

Furniture Index, http://www.furnitureindex.dk (accessed March 20, 2007).

Glambek, Ingeborg. "'One of the age's noblest cultural movements' On the theoretical basis for the Arts and Crafts Movement." *Scandinavian Journal of Design History 1* (1991): 47–76.

Goldberger, Paul. "Design Notebook." *New York Times*, September 30, 1982, Section C, 8.

Green, Penelope. "Mirror, Mirror; Marimekko, I Think I Love You." *New York Times*, May 21, 2000, Section 9, 2.

Hamilton, William L. "Design Notebook: What's Cool, Calm and Collected? Nordic Modern." *New York Times*, February 26, 1998, Section F, 1.

Henningsen, Poul. "Concerning a Shoehorn…" *Mobilia*, no. 54 (January 1960).

———. *Mobilia*, no. 56–57 (March-April 1960).

Hiort, Esborn. "Design and Function." *Danish Foreign Office Journal*, no. 62 (1968).

"Homemakers' Tastes Like Those of Buyers." *New York Times*, May 27, 1953, 36.

Huxtable, Ada Louise. "Danish Design: From Its Famous Past to the Present; The Melancholy Fate Of Danish Modern Style," *New York Times*, August 21, 1980, Home Section, C1.

Jepsen, Anton. *125 Years of Danish Furniture Making.* Rudolph Rasmussen. http://www.rudrasmussen.dk/Content/filead min/pdf/jubitekst.pdf (accessed February 20, 2007).

Klint, Esben. *Mobilia*, no. 55 (February 1960).

Knox, Sandra. "Long-Awaited Museum Show Opens; Spare Modern Style Takes Spotlight Among Arts." *New York Times*, October 15, 1960, Food Fashions Family Furnishings, 14.

Lelan, John. "The World of IKEA; A Prefab Utopia." *New York Times*, December 1, 2002, Design Magazine, Section 6, 92.

Louie, Elaine. "Danish Modern Is Hot." *New York Times*, October 6, 1994, Section C, 14.

———. "House Proud; When a Small Budget Thinks Big." *New York Times*, December, 29, 2005, Section F, 1.

"Made-by-Hand Campaign Is Opened." *New York Times*, June 10, 1964, 42.

"New Modern Pieces Are Heavy In Design." *New York Times*, April 3, 1950, 23.

O'Brien, George. "Danish Furniture Designs Rated Best at Fair in Cologne; New Forms Are Rounded." *New York Times*, January 31, 1964, Food Fashion Family Furnishings Section, 31.

———. "Modern Furniture Predominates In Model Rooms Opening Today; Rosewood Is Favored; Many Styles Imported." *New York Times*, July 17, 1964, Food Fashions Family Furnishings Section, 30.

Owens, Michael. "Reclining Dudes." *New York Times*, March 10, 2002, *The Times Magazine*, Section 6, 88.

Pepis, Betty "Bonniers Exhibits Swedish Articles; New Madison Ave. Store Opens With Hard-to-Find Items From Scandinavia." *New York Times*, October 9, 1948, 10.

Pepis, Betty. "Danish Collection of Furniture Here; Variety of Wood Used in Pieces That Are Put on Display by Swedish Modern." *New York Times*, March 5, 1952, 26.

———. "Designed In Denmark." New York Times, January 14, 1951, *The New York Times Magazine*, SM16.

———. "Foreign Furniture Easily Assembled; Swedish-Made Units Marked by Clean Lines and More Than Usual Comfort." *New York Times*, December 18, 1950, 26.

———. "For the Home: Danish Craft Designs Stem-From the Traditional; Display Shows Debt to 18th Century English Furniture." *New York Times*, July 15, 1950, 16.

———. "Good Design Goes International." New York Times, September 21, 1952, *The New York Times Magazine*, SM48.

———. "New Chair Styles Should Suit All; Jensen Has 84 Varieties on Hand, Including Dutch and Scandinavian." *New York Times*, February 16, 1955, 33.

———. "Small Budget, Big Results." *New York Times*, November 8, 1953, *The New York Times Magazine*, SM52.

Plumb, Barbara. "Dane Decries 'Backward' Furniture." *New York Times*, October 24, 1963, Real Estate Section, 29.

"Scandinavian Lamps and Furniture Shown." *New York Times*, October 12, 1950, 40.

"Scandinavian Shop Presents Variety of Teak Wall Units." *New York Times*, February 21, 1961, Food Fashions Family Furnishings Section, 38.

"Scandinavians Send New Batch of Furnishings." *New York Times*, November 21, 1957, Family/Style Section, 52.

"Showroom Stocks Teak For Conservatives Only; Scandinavian Designers Turning To Blond Wood in New Furniture." *New York Times*, July 9, 1963, Real Estate Section, 22.

"Six Years of Scandinavian Design in Review; Winners of Lunning Prizes Show Designs Done Since the Awards." *New York Times*, March 27, 1957, Family/Style Section, 34.

Skurka, Norma. "Danish Modern Is Classic." *New York Times*, October 17, 1971, *The New York Times Magazine*, SM96.

Slesin, Suzanne. "Danish Today: Beyond The Furniture Classics; A Guide to Shopping Sources." *New York Times*, August 21, 1980, The Home Section, C6.

"Sweden Sends U.S. Small Furniture; Scaled for Tiny Apartments Abroad, It Is Offered Here for Use by Children." *New York Times*, November 29, 1947, 16.

Rasmussen, Steen Eiler. "Modern Danish Design." *Journal of the Royal Society of Arts* XCVI, no. 4761 (January 30, 1948).

Reif, Rita. "Design Book is Reviewed." *New York Times*, October 31, 1963, 28.

———. "Cooper Union Museum Offers Danish Exhibition." *New York Times*, October 19, 1962, Family/Style Section, 22.

———. "International with a Nordic Accent." *New York Times*, June 12, 1968, 42.

———. "Refinements Mark New Collection of Scandinavian Furniture on View Here; Palisander Wood Is Used—Designer Is Indebted to Wife." *New York Times*, October 28, 1958, Food Fashions Family Furnishings Section, 30.

Roche, Mary. "New Ideas and Inventions." *New York Times*, March 13, 1949, SM58.

"The Training in Furniture Design at the Academy of Arts." *The Architect Magazine*, 1930.

"Upholstered Pieces Newly Arrived From Copenhagen." *New York Times*, May 24, 1952, 22.

Warren, Virginia Lee. "Rosewood, Unadorned, Enjoys Modern Revival." *New York Times*, September 3, 1964, Food Fashions Family Furnishings Section, 32.

Miscellaneous

Lincoln, William A. *World Woods in Color.* Fresno: Linden Publishing Co. Inc., 1986.

Photographers

Scott Thompson Photography
4820 N. Hermitage Apt. 2A
Chicago, IL 60640
773-919-9917
scott@scottthompsonphoto.com

Egon Douglas Photography
Chicago, IL
847-624-4683
info@egondouglas.com

David Rosenthall Photography
1932 South Halsted Suite No. 101
Chicago, IL 60608
773-791-9188
www.davidrosenthall.com

Matthew Millman Photography
261 Bradford Street
San Francisco, CA 94110
415-577-3200
matthew@matthewmillman.com

Andrew Hollingsworth
222 West Huron Street
Chicago, IL
312-440-9554
www.andrewhollingsworth.com

Index